El Oso (Bear) No More

The Shawn D. Moore Transformation Story
13 Keys that Changed My Life

by
Shawn D. Moore

Purpose Publishing
1503 Main Street #168 ✪ Grandview, Missouri
www.purposepublishing.com

El Oso No More
Copyright © 2018 by Shawn Moore
ISBN: 978-0-9997999-01

Editing by: Brian Gines and Frank Kresen
Book Cover Design: Chavos Buycks

For permission and requests,
write to the publisher:
1503 Main Street, #168, Grandview, MO 64030.

Author Inquiries may be sent to
shawnmooreministries@gmail.com

DEDICATION

This book is dedicated to the Moore, Rowe and Winters families, my cousin Daryl White and the Keoltzow neighborhood.

My thanks goes to Bible Baptist Church, and their Pastor Marvin Corr, along with Bannister Road Baptist Church, and their Pastor Dwight Scott, for the role you played in my life to help me transition from the streets to the man that I am today.

Special thanks to my beautiful, loving and supportive wife Jennifer Winters Moore. My appreciation goes to Roxane Johnson, Kathie Collins, Denise Timberlake, Risa Williams and Matthew Shaw. God has used you all greatly, not just in words but deeds, to help me complete what God has lead me to do. To God be all the glory.

Table of Contents

INTRODUCTION-**9**

DECISIONS-**17**

DUMB-**29**

DANGEROUS-**39**

CRAZY-**45**

ILLOGICAL-**53**

CHANCES-**59**

REAL-**67**

RELIABLE-**75**

RIDICULOUS-**81**

CLOSE-**85**

FRIENDS-**91**

HOPE-**97**

OUTRAGEOUS-**103**

LOYAL-**107**

BETRAYAL-**113**

PROTECTED-**121**

FAMILY-**127**

FOOLISH-**133**

INSANE-**139**

CHANGE-**151**

Shawn Moore

6

In the greatest book ever written, the author said, "One generation passeth away and another generation cometh; but the earth abideth forever."

"You must never be fearful about what you are doing when it is right." — Rosa Parks.

INTRODUCTION

L ocked up! Sent down the river, incarcerated, jailed, doin' time... So many young men have lost their freedom, and even more have lost their lives. Personally, I have lost a lot of friends to the streets. They either went to prison or died at a young age by the hands of gun violence. What advice would you give someone like me, who was or is headed in the direction of imprisonment?

My friends and I knew the risks involved in the type of life we were living, but we just did not believe or did not care about those risks. We became a part of violent crimes, guns, drugs, alcohol, sex, and the list goes on and on and on. It's a vicious cycle for many. They do their time and are released only to be back in jail within a year or less. Life is not lived but merely survived, and the future seems hopeless.

But all is *not* lost!

*Jack Canfield tells the story of a woman who was going to commit suicide. She was homeless and living on the streets. It was winter time, she was pregnant, depressed, and mentally ill, and she wasn't taking her meds. She would go to McDonald's and clean up when it was cold. She would go to the library to spend some time throughout the day. The only problem with going to the library is that you had to read books if you were going to stay. So, she walked into the library to stay warm, and she grabbed a book from the self-development section. Now before she went to the library, she was plotting how she was going to deliver her baby and then commit suicide. She planned to give her baby to one of her friends and have them call the police. She planned to throw herself in front of a train.

The book she picked up was a *Chicken Soup* book written by Jack Canfield. She read a story called *Puppies for Sale*. The story detailed a little boy, who went into the mall and saw a sign that read "Puppies for Sale." He asked the salesman how much would the puppies cost. The boy noticed that one of the puppies was limping. The boy showed interest in the puppy. The salesman discouraged him from buying that puppy because he was born like that. The boy was persistent on buying it, regardless of its condition. The salesman told him that he would give him the puppy. The boy still wanted to pay full price for the puppy — he saw value in it. The salesman didn't fully understand until the boy revealed that he, too, had a birth defect. He showed the salesman by lifting his pants leg. The woman reading the story was so moved by the love displayed for the puppy that she decided not to commit suicide. She knew that someone could love her as well.

The boy cared for that puppy because he could relate. I care about what is going on in these streets because I can relate. I know how it is to hustle, deal with haters. I hauled guns — I could have ended up in the grave or sending someone there at such a young age. I lived a hoggish lifestyle, doing my own thing, not giving any thought or regard to those around me.

Don't tell me that sharing a story cannot make a difference in someone's life. It has, and it will continue to do so. I want people in the streets to know that, if there was hope for me, then there is hope for everyone. There may be people who may not see the importance of me sharing my story. However, I am ever mindful of the words of Michael Jordan: "I can accept failure, everyone fails at something, but I cannot accept not trying."

To be successful, you must be willing to take chances. Michael Jordan said, "I've missed more than 9,000 shots in my career." He lost almost 300 games. He was trusted 26 times to take the game-winning shot, and he missed. He failed repeatedly in his life, and that is why he succeeded. I can't go to the grave without at least trying to make a difference in this world that we live in.

I went from living the street life to an exemplary life. It sure isn't fair for me to live the life that I am living and not share my story. I hope my story may turn someone's life from daily survival to one of real life.

I know we will not be able to bring an end to all the violence, crime, and other problems of the world, but we can try. We can try to bring an end to these problems one person at a time, if we are willing.

You might be thinking that I do not know anything about you. You may say that I cannot possibly know what it's like or what you have been through. However, I do know exactly what it's like — because I was in the same place! The street life! I was there! I lived it! I was in the same place you are now in or the same place someone you know is in. I was going down those same roads, making those same mistakes.

What do you think must happen in a person's life for them to decide it's time to change? For me, it was when I was going to kill my girlfriend of nine years and a few other people. Go to the White House, airport, or police station and say I am thinking about killing somebody. Let me know how that works out for you. No one has been murdered without someone thinking about it first. According to the Feminist Majority Foundation, the FBI reports that between 1976 and 1996, domestic violence claimed the lives of more than four women each day. I did not want to be one of those men spending time in prison because of domestic violence or being guilty of a black–on–black crime. I knew I had some issues when my thoughts were only to kill, destroy, finish, murder, annihilate, and terminate individuals' lives. I am so grateful that I realized I needed to change. I needed help with my attitude and anger.

In this book, I will tell you some of what I went through that led me to realize that I'd better change before I get locked up or end up dead. I was finally willing to change at the age of 28 but only after having made a lot of mistakes and living through a lot of regrets and missed opportunities.

I am not trying to paint a picture of me being tough, hardcore, or even perfect. I really don't believe in people being hard anymore unless they don't bleed. One day early in my life, I was having problems with this group of dudes, and I was afraid my little cousin, who was in the streets more than I was, told me not to worry about them because they bleed just like everyone else. I didn't fully understand what he meant by that statement until I got deeper into the game.

I am a living testimony that change is possible, no matter what choices you have made in the past. I am living proof that you do not have to be what you have always been or be like everyone else. You have a choice! In 1998, I made a choice that I was not going to continue to go down the same road or path that my life was headed. To my surprise, I'm now living rather than merely surviving. This is my story. The Shawn Moore Story.

It's never too late to change, no matter what you have done. In chapter 1, I will show you how some decisions I made opened the door for me to almost become a statistic.

The people in this book are real people, and all the stories are true. For privacy as well as liability issues, I have substituted the names of my friends with the names of animals.

"It doesn't matter where you are coming from. All that matters is where you are going" — Brian Tracy

1

DECISIONS

I want you to better understand where I came from in order for you to understand my story and what is so extraordinary about where I am today. We must start at the beginning of my life. I was born on November 7, 1970, and grew up in Saginaw, Michigan. I lived with both of my biological parents along with my sister and brother. It was in Saginaw, Michigan, where my dad met my mother. My parents were married in 1971 and are still together today.

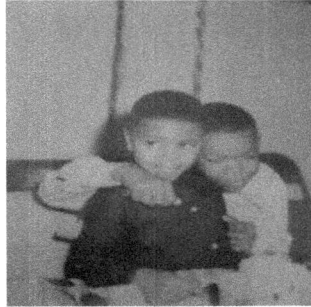

My mother was one of sixteen children, with one sibling dying at birth. She and her remaining fourteen siblings grew up in Alabama in a house with only one bathroom! Can you imagine all of those people, all of those kids, and only one bathroom in the entire house? Mom is the most quietest, content, patient, grateful, giving, and loving woman I have ever met in my life. My mom was the best domestic engineer I know.

My father, while living in Louisiana, lost his mother, my grandmother, his two sisters, and a brother in a house fire. Imagine: In one day, my Dad's world turned upside-down at the tender age of six. After that tragedy, his father, my grandfather, relocated his family to Saginaw, Michigan, where he found work at a manufacturing plant. When my father became of age, he joined the U.S. Army. Afterwards, he followed in my grandfather's footsteps and worked in one of the many car-manufacturing plants in the Saginaw area. Dad is a calm, outgoing, caring, generous, and hardworking man.

Hopefully, after reading the characteristics of these two people who raised me, you can understand how my personality was formed and the way I think. I rarely ever saw my parents upset except when dealing with their disobedient children, which were usually my sister and me. (My little brother was usually the innocent one in the family.)

My parents still live in Saginaw today. My sister lives in the Detroit area, and my brother relocated to Alabama. I currently live in Kansas City, Missouri. According to the 2013 United States Census, the city's population was 467,007. Kansas City (known as killer city) is ranked number 34 out of 100 of America's Most Dangerous Cities to live. That is interesting because the place where I grew up has a high crime rate as well.

Let me tell you about Saginaw, Michigan (known as Sagnasty). It is about 100 miles north of Detroit. There was a time when you could make a good living working in the automotive industry, which is what most people who lived in Saginaw did. As years passed, one by one, the plants closed, and unemployment skyrocketed. When unemployment increases, socioeconomic problems related to poverty increase, which leads to high crime rates and includes but is not limited to crimes against persons and property.

According to the United States Census of 1970, the year I was born, the population of Saginaw was 220,419. In 1990, 20 years later, the population dropped to 69,536, and, in 2010, the population decreased to 50,303. Since 2010, Saginaw has ranked in the Top 10 on the list of America's Top 100 Most Dangerous Cities to live in. According to *Neighborhood Scout*, in 2014, Saginaw, Michigan, was ranked 4th as being the most dangerous city to live.

To put that in perspective, Saginaw is as dangerous a place to live in as Oakland, California, Detroit, Flint, Michigan, East St. Louis, and Chicago, Illinois. According to the area's crime statistics, a person has a 1 in 50 chances of becoming the victim of a crime in Saginaw. These dreary and depressing statistics might lead some to believe that if you live in Saginaw, you will not amount to much. There is a high probability that a Saginaw, Michigan, resident may not graduate from high school, may indeed visit the criminal justice system more than once, probably join a gang, experiment with and/or become addicted to drugs, and probably have a drinking problem.

Some residents living in Saginaw or other comparable cities might believe there is no point in trying to better yourself. If you come from Saginaw or any other city like it, you may get the idea you cannot be successful because there is too much stacked against you, or the odds are not in your favor. Do you know of any successful people who were born in Saginaw, Michigan? You may be able to name a few; however, there are several famous and successful people born and raised in Saginaw. Stevie Wonder and Serena Williams were both born in Saginaw, Michigan. Then Pittsburgh Steelers now Arizona Cardinals linebacker Lamar Woodley, former pro-football player Charles Rogers, former pro-basketball players Jason Richardson and Mark Macon, and Golden State Warriors forward Draymond Green were born and raised in Saginaw. There are many others — professional athletes, actors, successful entrepreneurs, inventors, authors, and musicians — who once made their home in Saginaw.

*Les Brown said, "Other people's opinion of you does not have to become your reality." The point I am trying to make is that where you were born or where you were raised does not determine the type of person you can become. Saginaw, Michigan, was not and is not an easy place to live. This city, like other metropolitan areas, has victims of unemployment, high crime rates, gangs, drugs, and alcoholism. These problems have touched everyone, directly and indirectly, in one way or the other. Escaping from these problems is what most people try to pursue every day. Unfortunately, like the lyrics of an old country song, "Looking for love in all the wrong places," by Johnnie Lee, they were looking in all the wrong places. If you do not have a musical talent like Stevie Wonder or an athletic ability like Serena Williams, you must find another way to succeed or rise out of the problems that plague Saginaw, Michigan.

I was smart and an athlete who played basketball, soccer, and baseball. But rather than applying myself in school or using sports as a way out, I was too focused on trying to fit in and be cool. I was not unintelligent, but as you read this book, I will show you how intelligent people can make some foolish decisions. So, I turned to drugs, alcohol, and women as my means of escape. By "escape," I don't necessarily mean the physical act of leaving the area. Oftentimes, I was trying to escape the feeling of not belonging and living up to the expectations of society. All I really wanted was to be loved and accepted, and I felt the streets provided that for me. In the streets, I wanted to be respected by my friends and my enemies. I wanted "street creds" and was almost willing to do just about whatever it took to get them.

Like most kids in Saginaw, I attended public school. At age ten, I was being bullied at school. To protect me, my parents transferred me to a private school. Unfortunately, the move to a private school did not resolve anything. In the 1980s, here I was a black kid from "the hood" attending a predominantly white private school! Although my parents meant well, they basically traded one set of problems for another. I felt like a zebra running from a lion. The zebra jumps into the water to escape the lion, only to get eaten by a crocodile.

Therefore, my problems of being bullied followed me to the private school. At the private school, I rebelled against authority. At the age of 15, I was drinking alcohol. At the age of 16, I started to smoke weed, experiment with sex, sneaking around and carrying my dad's gun.

To say that I got into trouble is an understatement. I got myself expelled, kicked out of that special, unique, and predominantly white private school during my senior year of high school. Let's be clear here: I could have easily said, "I got kicked out" giving the impression that it was not my fault, at least not all of it. I could have added that the administrators of that school didn't care about me and were out to get me because I am black. But that would not have been the truth. Dr. Robert Anthony said, "When you blame others, you give up your power to change." No single drop of water thinks it is responsible for the flood. I have learned, as G Batiste said, the ones who take ownership of their lives are likely to be more successful. At some point in your life, you must stop playing the blame game and own up to your dumb decisions.

I must admit that I got myself kicked out because I was caught smoking weed, drinking, and messing with the girls when I knew it was against the rules. It didn't matter if the rules were fair or not. I knew what the rules were, and all I had to do was to obey them and graduate. Simple! But I made a choice and decided that what I wanted to do was more important than what they did not want me to do. I was rebellious and childish, and certainly did not like people in positions of authority telling me what to do. Sound familiar? Imagine how my life could have been if I had decided to listen to the authority in my life and followed the rules. I would have graduated on time and most likely would have avoided a lot of problems I had. I am still suffering the consequences from some of the decisions I made. I am happy with how my life has turned out. But, I must be honest: I still have a lot of regrets.

Here I was, in my senior year, returning to the public school feeling abashed. To make matters worse, all my class credits from the private school did not transfer to the public school. This meant that for me to graduate, I had to attend another full school year. Now I was back in a predominantly black school with the same kids from the same neighborhood. All of them knew I'd left to attend a private school. They knew I was the same age as they were and should be graduating with them, but I was not! Yes, I had to explain why I was back and why I was not graduating. *Dr. Willie Joley says, "A setback is a set up for a comeback," and I did not let that setback stop me from graduating from high school. According to *statisticbrain.com*, 90% of jobs require a high school diploma, and 75% of crimes are committed by a high school dropout. I didn't want to be a high school dropout because I knew I would be at a greater risk of getting in trouble. So, I did what I had to do to make sure I walked across that stage to get my diploma. That was one of only a few good choices I made during that time.

Furthermore, I had to prove that I did not think of myself as better than everyone else because I had attended a private school. Also, I had to prove to everyone that I was not "soft." So, I started bragging about why I got kicked out. I started hanging out with the kids from the neighborhood every day, whereas in the past, it was occasionaly. Before transferring to the private school, I had attended Keoltzow Elementary School, where I got to know all the kids from my neighborhood. Now I was attending Buena Vista High School with the same kids who'd attended Keoltzow. We automatically had enemies because of the area in which we lived. I thought it was unfair since I had no choice in the matter of where I lived, but I still had to deal with the consequences daily.

Have you ever made a choice, and, at the time, you thought it was your only option, only later to find out you had other options? In my mind, I had to connect with the guys in my neighborhood. What was unfortunate for me was that a lot of them were involved in the street life. I knew people who' steered clear from that lifestyle, who weren't doing drugs or in the streets. We called them "squares," "jocks," or "outcasts." The fear of not being accepted was harder to overcome than the fear of living life in the streets. Now that I am older, I realize that life is hard — no matter what road you choose. It brought comfort to me to hang around my friends in my neighborhood with that common factor that held us together. We all had the same enemies based on the side of town we lived on. I knew they had my back, and I quickly learned I needed to have theirs as well. At age seventeen, nothing felt worse than being an outcast, so I began doing what my friends were doing just to fit in.

During that time in my life and for many years to come, my biggest fear was not going to jail or even dying. I feared being alone, being put down, spoken of in a negative way and not being considered one of the guys. I feared having no friends and not being thought of as being "cool." Those fears formed the foundation of the many bad decisions I would soon make.

I believe that there is a basic desire within every human being to be accepted and included in a group of friends. No one likes to be on the outside looking in, and so you search for a way to be accepted into the group where you think the fun is. The only problem with that mindset is what may be fun for today can and usually does result in heartache, pain, and regrets tomorrow. I can drive this point home in less than 10 words. *Remember Len Bias, who was one of the greatest.* I was trying so hard to fit in and trying so hard to make a name for myself that it almost cost me my freedom — not to mention my life.

In Chapter 2, I will show you how a few *dumb* decisions almost cost me my life and how, if I would have went home to get my guns, I may have been in jeopardy of losing my freedom.

"You gain strength, courage, and confidence by every experience in which you really stop to look fear in the face. You must do all the things which you think you cannot do." —
Eleanor Roosevelt

2

DUMB

This day was nothing special. I was 20 years old, at work, and my phone rang. I wasn't supposed to answer my phone on the job, but I did — and, boy, I wish I hadn't. Tension and apprehension ran through my veins as I heard a familiar voice on the other end of the phone yelling and screaming at me.

My mind quickly raced back to about a month prior, when my friend Cat, who reminds me of Morris Chestnut. He was a smooth fellow; he was calling me to hang out with some friends. Cat was already with them, so I just went along with the program. It was dumb for me not to listen to my conscience when I found out that Snake and Gorilla would not be with us, even though their girlfriends came to hang out with us. Snake was one of my good friends from the neighborhood. We were like Kane and O-Dog in *Menace to Society*; we were tight and always together. Gorilla was cool, but I had known him for only a year or two.

Both girls were fine, good looking. So, I succumbed to temptation. We hung out and had a good time. I was enjoying myself. I was spending time with Gorilla's girlfriend. The night ended with us messing around. I didn't think much of it. It was a one-time thing.

A month later, here I am on the phone with Gorilla yelling and screaming at me, "How could you mess with my girl? I thought we were cool." I was shocked that he'd found out, and, immediately, fear kicked in, and ice ran through my system. I already had enough enemies, and I was trying not to add any more to that list, but it seemed too late for that not to happen.

In the early '90s, most people did not have large-caliber handguns unless they had a lot of money. Gorilla had a nine-millimeter, and all I had was a 38 and a 380. I was at work, and my guns were at home. My job was in Bridgeport, Michigan, one minute from the state police headquarters. They had a tendency to pull people over just to check them out. So, I rarely took my guns to work because of the possibility of getting pulled over and my car being searched.

Gorilla was staying with my friend Tiger at the time. During this phone conversation, Gorilla asked me to meet him at Tiger's house after I got off work. He wanted to talk to me about what had happened between me and his girl. I knew I was not in a good situation either way. My conscience told me to think through my choices. I could have called some of my friends to go with me, but then it would have appeared I was afraid to face him alone, and I didn't want anyone thinking I was afraid.

I could have decided to go home to get my guns first, but I wanted him to know that I came directly from work — letting him know I wasn't stalling. I was as real as they came, ready to face whatever came. If I wanted to earn respect in the streets, this was a part of the process. That process started with me believing I was hard before anyone else would know I was.

I knew I was wrong. You should never mess with a man's girl. I wouldn't want anyone to disrespect me like that. My actions were disrespectful, so I understood why Gorilla was so angry. Have you ever done anything that you later regretted? This is one of those decisions that I regretted later.

My conscience was bothering me after the phone call ended. Choices ran through my head, and I could not concentrate on work. I was faced with a tough decision: Do I go over there and face the consequences from my horrible decision, or do I avoid him and let him, and everyone else, think I was afraid to face him? There was no way I could take the risk of him telling people I was scared to come talk to him.

This is what was running through my mind: If I did not go, he would think I was a punk. If I did go, he might kill me, or I might have to kill him. Either way, it was a lose/lose situation. I had about three hours, before leaving work, to decide what to do. I decided to go straight from work, without my guns.

I wanted my guns with me! Wait. Gorilla did not know whether I had my guns or not. Everybody knew I kept a gun on me. I had to face my fears. I did not know what was going to happen. While driving over to Tiger's house, I thought this could quite possibly be my last day on this earth.

I was so afraid when I arrived at Tiger's house. My heart was pounding out of my chest. I felt as though I was having a heart attack. My ears were ringing. Gorilla was waiting outside for me. He had this displeased and enraged look on his face. When I got out of the car, his expression changed to a look of surprise. It was as though he couldn't believe I would show up. We talked cordially. Soon, I noticed that it was becoming arduous, difficult for him to talk to me. He became so angry that he began to tremble while he spoke. His eyes became darker and could not stand still. Shortly afterwards, one of his friends pulled up. I said to myself, *This isn't good*. Now it was the three of us, and Gorilla wanted us to go inside the house.

I did not want to go inside because his demeanor and the tone of his voice had changed. He had become a different person. He started getting louder. Was Gorilla trying to impress his friend? He had a dangerous, killer look in his eyes. His pupils dilated, and he started to sweat rage from his pores. Again, I knew I was wrong. Again, I wondered how that day would end. The only certainty for me was that I was not going to show any signs of weakness. So, as my pulse pounded out of control, I went into the house with a cool demeanor.

Gorilla had already told his friend what had happened between me and his girlfriend. He expressed again how I was wrong and that I was lucky that he was not going to do anything to me. I was so relieved to hear those words. He showed his gun and said if he wanted to kill me, he could. When he was finished putting me in my place, he told me to leave. I couldn't leave that house fast enough.

When I got in my car, I couldn't believe that I was still alive. The tension inside me had built to a point where all I could do was laugh, and it was uncontrollable. Cold sweat dried on my skin, and I felt as though I just finished riding the Blue Streak at Cedar Point. Cedar Point is an amusement park in Sandusky, Ohio. I would have said the Magnum, but that would have been a lie because I was afraid then — and even now — to ride that roller coaster. I had survived another day and conquered my fear of dying or being killed by a man. I had faced my fear of being shot. I knew that Gorilla had a gun and that he was mad at me for messing with his girl. I had to swallow the fact that I made a bad decision, and bad consequences come with bad decisions. I took the bull by the horns. To some, going into the house was the bravest decision. To others, that was the dumbest decision ever made. Remember, I had chosen the path of street life, which comes with good and bad consequences for the decisions we make. So, whether it be jail or death, I was willing to suffer the consequences. In my mind, it was all good. I know — that was just dumb thinking. However, in this game, for me, there was no faking it.

The fear of not being accepted by my peers led me to face my fear of dying and deal with it once and for all.

What is fear keeping you from doing? Are you afraid to try to change because of fear of failing? Are you running from the results of bad choices, or are you blaming others rather than owning up to it yourself? Are you afraid to make different choices because of what someone else might think or say?

Not all fear is bad. Most times, fear is a good thing to have, as it makes us think and evaluate our circumstances before doing something we shouldn't. Fear of killing someone, being killed, and going to prison for the rest of our lives are good fears to have.

But it is fear that cripples you and keeps you from doing what is right, from making better choices, from dreaming you can do better in life than what you are doing. Remember that some fears are good, but a fear of change is not one of them. A fear of change keeps us from becoming what we want to be or can be.

What are you fearful of today? If you say "Nothing," that's not a good answer. Keep in mind: Not all fear is bad. I wish now I would have feared disappointing the people who really loved me more than I did. I hurt my mom and dad more than I care to think about. At the time, I didn't listen to or care about the people who really loved me and wanted me to do something with my life.

What about you? I know someone may be saying, "I didn't have a mom and dad," but if you look hard enough, you had someone in your life who loves you and cares for you and has given you good advice. I challenge you: Don't be like me. I allowed fear to cause me to make some very dumb decisions.

My goal was to not have anyone think I was weak — none. From that moment on, any decisions I made could cost me my life or my freedom. That became the norm in my life: To become the person I was trying to be — *hard*.

I don't believe it was a coincidence that I survived not being killed that day. As you continue to read my story in Chapter 3, I will show you how *dangerous* my life was becoming and why I fell in love with carrying guns.

"I don't go looking for trouble. Trouble usually finds me." — Katie McGarry

3

DANGEROUS

Death is not something you want to wake up thinking about. Even though we all know we must die one day, it is hard to get your brain to wrap around that concept. On this day, I was not thinking about dying at the young age of 21. I was trying to get high. So, I went to my friend Anaconda's house. It was OK to smoke weed there. My friend Snake went with me. Anaconda had company. A girl from the neighborhood was there. Anaconda was not dating her. She was a cool friend with all of us. Anaconda noticed her talking to me a lot, and, out of jealousy, he asked me to leave. I got mad because Snake, who'd come with me, was not asked to leave — just me! I don't remember what I said to him, but, whatever I said, he didn't like it.

Anaconda challenged me to go outside and fight. He asked me to put my gun down and fight him. Like I said before, everybody knew I had a gun on me, and I did. The only reason I started carrying guns is because people had stopped fighting and started shooting. It used to be where two guys would get into a fight and you would live to fight another day. But times were changing, and people were dying. And I wasn't trying to be one of those who got killed. When the wintertime comes in Michigan, you'd better put your coat on. The streets were changing, and, therefore, I adapted to my environment and added a gun to my wardrobe.

Anaconda did not know that my parents had signed me up for karate lessons while I was attending the private school. I had gotten pretty good with defending myself with my bare hands. There was this one kid at the private school who loved the military, and, for some reason, he always picked on me, and we fought often. Over the years, I got lots of experience fighting with him and others.

So, I gladly accepted Anaconda's invitation to put my gun down and fight him. I took my gun out of my pocket and placed it on top of the car. As I was squaring off to fight him, he quickly pulled my winter hat down over my eyes. I could not see anything. I was ready to fight, and now I'd been tricked. Seeing nothing but darkness for a split second, I became alarmed. Apparent dread ran through me, as though a panic attack was heading my way. Suddenly I felt his hands near my waist. In that second, I knew where he was positioned — directly in front of me. I braced myself, ready to get hit in the face. Instead of wasting valuable seconds in removing my cap, I swung. Hard.

I did not know where my punch landed, but I knew I'd made contact because a dull ache coursed through my knuckles. I lifted my hat and saw he was on the ground. I'd hit him so hard that he took one look at me, got up, and ran inside the house. I thought it was over until I saw him coming out of the door with a long kitchen knife. I reached for my gun. It was gone. I did what any real man would do. I ran. I ran hard and as fast as I could, not looking back at all.

I ran around the corner to Snake's house and banged on the door. His mom let me in, and I was glad she did. I phoned Snake, who was still at Anaconda's house, to see if he had my gun. He did, so I asked him to bring my gun to his house.

A few minutes later, there was a knock at the door. I opened it, and Anaconda was standing there. I quickly slammed the door in his face, agitated that it was not Snake, and waited for him to bring my gun. Truthfully, I was apprehensive because Snake was a friend to both of us. I didn't know if Snake was going to give Anaconda my gun or bring my gun to me. In the streets, you must be on guard for anything. I don't know what Anaconda did when I slammed the door in his face, and truthfully, I didn't care. All I wanted was my gun.

When Snake arrived, I asked him why he'd taken my gun. He said he did not want me to shoot Anaconda. He asked me what I would have done if I had my gun. I told him, "You already know." But I do remember telling him that I didn't really want to shoot Anaconda. But if he would have tried to stab me with that knife, what was I to do? I was petrified of being stabbed with a knife.

After evaluating the entire incident, I realized what Anaconda's hands were doing near my waist. He may have been reaching for the bottom of my coat to pull it up over my head while I was trying to remove my hat from my eyes. This strategy would have given him the advantage over me, and I would have been blind and bound. Smart.

You see, Anaconda was from the old school and had spent time in prison. He weighed about 165 — picture JJ on *Good Times* but with about 20 more pounds, compared to my 275 pounds. He knew he could not have fought me equally. He had to have an advantage, an upper hand.

Looking back, I am grateful to Snake for taking my gun away, because this story could have had an entirely different ending. However, after that day, I never put my gun down to fight anyone ever again. I stayed strapped.

Facing death that day taught me not to trust anyone. Anaconda was one of my friends from the neighborhood, but, because of a female, suddenly my life was in danger, again. I don't believe it was a stroke of luck that Snake took my gun that day. I think it's odd that Anaconda didn't catch me. Even though I was running fast, I don't think I was running *that* fast. I don't know how far he chased me with that knife. Like I said, I didn't look back at all until I got to the door of Snake's home.

In Chapter 4 I will show you how *crazy* my way of thinking had developed and how someone driving down a street could have changed the course of my life.

"Relationships are about trust, and, if you have to play detective in your relationship, then it's time to move on." — Unknown

4

CRAZY

The time came for me to do what I really wanted and needed to do to get the respect I wanted in the streets. There were a few times in my life that I was going to kill someone. This was one of those times.

I was going to see my girlfriend of three years. I was about 22 years old at the time. While I was pulling up her driveway, I saw a car leaving. I asked her who was leaving, and she said that they were at the wrong house. She said they thought a party was going on. It sounded suspicious, but I did not think much more about it that night.

A month later, I caught the same car in her driveway again. Before they pulled out I blocked the car from leaving. I got out, went to the car, and asked who they were and why they were there — even though I already knew the answers to the questions I was asking. One guy said something smart instead. I got angry. It was like heat building up inside me, wanting to be let free. I thought to myself, *You're getting smart, and you're at my girl's house.* I told him, "Please, don't get smart with me right now. My head is not in a good place right now!" I lifted my shirt, showed him my gun, turned, and went back to my car. I was angrier with her than them. I got into my car and left as I got a sick feeling in my gut.

The guy and his friend chased me down the street. I was thinking, *I am about to shoot this dude!* as my muscles tightened. He pulled his car up beside mine. I rolled down the window to see what he had to say. He told me his side of the story. He told me that my girlfriend told him that she didn't have a man. I told him, "It's all good, then — just a misunderstanding." I went home to clear my head.

Let me tell you this: Saginaw, Michigan is a small town. If you ride around a lot, like I did, you are bound to see people sooner or later. So, I was just riding around, and I saw Ant. He looked at me and smiled. I said to myself, *No, he didn't.* I gave him a pass that day. The next time I saw him, he did the same thing. This time I had my boys with me. I hit a U-turn and followed him.

Snake was in the car with me. After noticing what I'd just done, he asked me what was up. I told him, "That's the dude I caught over at my girl's house." My friends Cat and Python were in a car following behind us. When I caught up to Ant, he was on the corner of Genessee and Weber, buying fireworks. By the time I got to him, he was back in his car with one of his boys.

I got out of my car and ran up to his car window. I asked him, "Ant, what's up with this smiling every time you see me?" He told me he could smile at anyone he wanted to. I told him that was true. I also told him not to blame me for what was going to happen if he continued to disrespect me. Every time I saw him, he had this smug look on his face as if to say, "I've been with your girl." Before I knew it, he reached under his seat, and my instinct was that he was reaching for a gun. I quickly ran back to my car to get my guns. Ant pulled off. Snake, Cat, Python, and I did not chase him. One reason for my decision was that it was daylight. Another reason: too many witnesses saw the confrontation. The last reason was that I really wasn't trying to go to jail that day.

Later that night, my girlfriend said Ant did not have a gun but was reaching for a machete. I told her that she'd let me down and had put my life in danger. I was all about making money and staying low-key. I told her that she'd jeopardized all of that and that the situation was about to get ugly.

I know you're wondering why I was still with my girlfriend when it seemed as if she were cheating. I can sum it up in one word: Crazy. I was crazy to think that the relationship would someday change. She had told me over and over she wasn't going to be like my momma and stay at home. But that was exactly what I was looking for: A Domestic Engineer, a stay-at-home mom. I believe that should be one of the most respected positions in the world and should not be looked down upon. I wanted to start a family one day and settle down, but there were some things this girl could do better than others that kept me tangled up in this relationship. Deep down inside, I wanted it to work out, but I knew it wouldn't.

One evening, my girlfriend went to the store and I was at her house chillin,' smoking some weed, and waiting for her to return. Her phone rang. I answered it, and it was Ant. He called me stupid for being over there. I told him to come over to see how stupid I was. I was already high, not thinking clearly, mind clouded. I lit another joint and left the house with the front door open. I walked across the street smoking a joint with my guns in my hand. I left my car in her driveway.

There were some bushes across the street, so I hid in them to wait for my target. I called a friend who lived eight houses down the street and told him what I was planning to do. I told him that, after I'd finished this business, I would run to his house to hide out. I've heard it said that best friends are people you don't need to talk to every single day. You could go for weeks without talking to them, but when you do, it's as if you'd never stopped talking. This was one of those friends. I was so high that I did not realize that the killing I was planning would be solved by the cops easily. My mind was not hitting on all cylinders. My car was in the driveway, and I'd left the front door open.

That moment, I was so angry that a black hole of emotions consumed me. I didn't care. I was in the dark, lying in wait in the bushes, smoking a joint, ready for him to come, so that I could end his life. Every car's headlights I saw coming my way raised my already-erratic heartbeat. Then I saw him, and my heart was pounding so hard it felt like heavy hail beating on my chest. I watched as he drove. What did he do? He never turned down into the street where my girlfriend lived. He did not turn and drive down the street where I was waiting to kill him. He drove past the turn.

Now, as I'm writing this story, I'm glad Ant didn't turn down the street where I was waiting for him. If he had come down the street, I know I would have killed him or at least unloaded my guns trying. My goal at that time was to kill him. Hear what I am about to say: I was high and I thought I saw my man's car. Still, to this day, I don't really know for sure if it was him or not. But whoever was driving that car was probably going to get shot that night. Crazy thinking leads to crazy actions, with little regard for the consequences of our decisions. What made this whole situation even more ironic was that I saw Ant only one more time in my whole life. I don't know what happened to him. Did he move? Was he dead? In prison? I look back now, and I am so grateful that I didn't get the opportunity to do what I had planned to do that night. I don't believe it's a coincidence that I saw him only one more time in my life and his car had not come down the street.

I was astonished at the person I had become. I was beginning to have very little respect for human life. Deep down inside, I knew that this feeling, this thought, was not a good thing. But, I was in the game, and there was no turning back. That fear of someone killing me only gave me a stronger desire to shoot first and ask questions later. That night was one of those nights. I was ready to do whatever was necessary to get respect.

Do you think the decisions I had been making were wise or foolish? What do you think about the decisions you or someone you know are currently making? Are they wise or foolish? Where are your choices in life taking you this very moment?

Can you see how crazy my life was turning out? In Chapter 5, I will show you how I almost died from *illogical* thinking and impersonating a collection agent.

"Make somebody happy today, and mind your own business." — Ann Landers

5

ILLOGICAL

One evening I was hanging out with my friends Cat and Cobra. Cobra was Cat's cousin, and he was the man. Cobra was the one who introduced me to selling crack cocaine. Cobra thought he was Nino Brown, the godfather and big drug kingpin. He had big dreams. Cat, who was his cousin and my good friend from the neighborhood, and I were going to help him reach his dreams. I was about 23 years old at the time.

I loved hanging around Cobra because he had a business mindset, and he loved having things — nice cars, sounds, clothes, shoes, and jewelry. My kind of man. One thing about me, even though I needed attention and had a strong need to be accepted by my friends, I had my limits. They say money doesn't bring you happiness, but I say, "Neither does being broke." That was my philosophy in the streets.

I had some friends who just loved getting high. They would spend every dime they had to get high. Sometimes they would steal from family and friends just to get high. I loved money and women too much for all that. I loved looking good, having nice things like clothes, shoes, jewelry, and a nice car — and definitely money. I had to be around some females eventually. I couldn't stand just sitting in a room with men all day, getting high. In my mind, I was never going to be broke. Therefore, even though I was a hustler, I always worked a job, most of the time two. The jobs I took gave me the freedom to live the lifestyle I was living. Most of the time I was even selling drugs on my job, too. I am proud of the fact that I started working at the age of 16 and have never stopped working. I have always had a strong work ethic. My first job was in the fields with my Hispanic friends, and we had to start early in the morning.

Even when I was out all night, I rarely called in to work to ask for the day off. I loved the fact that people could depend on me. Therefore, Cat and Cobra recruited me to help them achieve their agenda. Even when I was in the streets, I lived a life of integrity — except when it came to women.

Cobra had a circle of people he would give dope to on credit all through the month. At the first of every month, we would go to collect the money they owed — plus the interest. A $20 credit would end up being $35 or more. So, you can imagine how much money we were collecting on the first of every month. These people were getting high every day. Business was good, including the transactions we took care of personally on a day-to-day basis all through the month.

Well, that day Cobra told me and Cat about this man who would not pay him his money. The man was married to Cobra's sister. In this business no, free favors were allowed. So, we went over to his sister's house to rough up her husband a bit.

Now, Cat is a strong dude. He had a 50-Cent type of body. When he hit you, it would hurt. I weighed 275 and thought I was all that because of my size. When her husband let us into the house, we grabbed him, threw him up against the kitchen cupboards, slapped him around a bit, and told him we weren't playing. We told him he better give Cobra his money — or else. Eventually, he paid Cobra his money.

Months later, Cat, Cobra and I were hanging out at Cobra's sister's house. I was rolling up a joint when Cobra's pager went off. He and Cat left to go around the corner to do a quick run. I stayed behind to roll joints. I had left my gun at home because hanging with Cobra was risky, because we always had a lot of dope on us. So, I never felt comfortable having my gun on me when I was in the truck with him. So, when I tell you that I kept my head down you'll understand why I reacted the way I did.

Cobra was fearless. He played his music so loud and didn't even care about the police, which I thought was crazy because we were always riding dirty. Back then the police would use the excuse of your music being too loud to pull you over all the time. So, this is why I stayed behind to roll up joints. While I was rolling joints, I saw something out of the corner of my eye. It was Cobra's brother-in-law. I should have known better. At the time, my heart dropped because I knew I was slipping. I was mad at myself because I always had my gun on me, and I knew better. My heart was beating like it does when something runs out in front of your car unexpectedly and you must slam on the brakes. This man was a Vietnam vet, and he had this old gun in his hand. Here I was — in *his* house — and he was about to get away with killing me.

He looked at me and said, "Where are your boys now?" Remember, they were all related, but I wasn't. I was an outsider in his eyes. I thought about trying to apologize just to get out of the house, but something told me not to say anything and, as a matter of fact, not even to look at him.

So I kept my head down and kept rolling joints as if he weren't there. It worked. When I looked up, he was gone. I knew he was still in the house somewhere, so I did not leave my seat until Cobra and Cat came back. I told them what had happened, and they laughed. They laughed hard. I did not think it was funny at all — especially since I didn't get any pay for beating him up. Here I was, facing death once more. I think it was illogical for me to believe it was okay to even go back over there after we had just roughed up the guy.

* Bruce Lee said, "Mistakes are always forgivable, if one has the courage to admit them. Remember — the only reason I am sharing my story is to provide hope for the next generation. If I can change, anybody can change. I don't believe that it was only good fortune that Cobra's brother-in-law did not kill me that day.

In Chapter 6, I will show you how me taking a chance changed my life entirely.

"It's impossible," said Pride. "It's risky," said Experience. "It's pointless," said Reason. "Give it a try," whispered the Heart." – Unknown

6

CHANCES

Zig Ziglar said, "Choices, chances, changes. You must make a choice to take a chance, or your life will never change." In 1998, I decided I needed to change. I wasn't happy with where my life was headed. There were very few times that I was sober, but in those times, I used to daydream about living a better life. I always wanted a house and a family. Yes, I could have had that at the time I was in the streets, but it would have made no sense to get married because all I would have done was cheat on my wife when things didn't go my way. Purchasing a home wouldn't have made sense either,

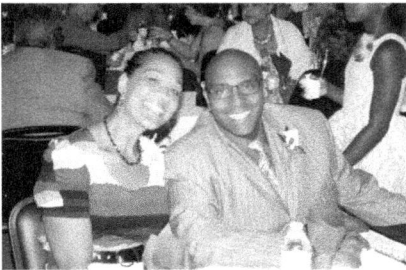

because I was selling drugs, and it was just a matter of time when the police or feds would one day kick in my door and take everything I had worked hard for in the streets and relocate my place of residence quickly.

So, when I decided to change, I decided to change. I know this is going to sound crazy, but the first goal that I had was to stop selling and doing drugs. The second goal was to leave these women alone. I decided "No more disrespecting women." I wasn't going to take advantage of women anymore. I wasn't going to use women to fulfill my selfish desires. That decision was one of the hardest decisions I ever made. Here I was, 28 years old, saying I would not have sex again until I got married. I could be wrong, but I believe a lot of the problems we have in the world today are because of family dynamics. Very few love themselves enough to wait for someone who is disciplined and committed to the relationship. Too many "settle," like I did, for years. According to a report released by the Urban Institute, the state of the African-American family is worse today than it was in the 1960s.

In 1950, 17 percent of African-American children lived in a home with their mother but not their father. By 2010, that had increased to 50 percent. In 1965, only 8 percent of childbirths in the black community occurred out of wedlock. In 2010, that figure was 41 percent, and, today, the out-of-wedlock childbirth in the black community sits at an astounding 72 percent. The number of African-American women married and living with their spouse was recorded as 53 percent in 1950. By 2010, it had dropped to 25 percent.

To change these stats, we need men who are disciplined and committed to marriage and their families. Discipline doesn't start when you get married. If you can't control yourself *before* you get married, you are going to have a hard time in your marriage. I always wanted to have a successful marriage, so I was committed to changing my ways so that, when I found the right woman, I would know how to treat her.

The whole point of me being so committed is because I wanted to be in the home. I wanted to be a husband and a father — even with the odds against me. Based on the statistics I just gave you, I knew I wanted to follow in my dad's footsteps and be there in the home for my kids and wife.

So, I went two years without having sexual intercourse, and I messed up and went to see one of my ex-girlfriends, thinking I was strong enough to say "No," but I messed up. After that day, I went 10 years without having sex. During those 10 years I met my wife. This year, we will be celebrating seven years of marriage, which is so cool because we spent seven years just being friends and talking on the phone just about life. Our conversations were not about "I like you — do you like me?" We were strictly friends all the way up to 2009, when I asked her if she was dating anyone, and she said, "No." I knew then she was going to be my wife. My wife was a 33-year-old virgin when I married her. She grew up in a God-fearing home with her four siblings. Her dad was a deacon and her mom a godly woman, so when she told me she was a virgin, I was surprised — but not that surprised. It was at that time that I realized making wise decisions and taking a chance produced good results. Here I was, a man who'd made a lot of mistakes. But I decided to make a hard decision at the age of 28, and, 12 years later, I was reaping the benefits from taking a chance. My wife and I had been married for about a year when the phone rang and the voice on the other end said, "You are dead the next time I see you." I didn't know who it was. I didn't know if it was work related, someone from the past, or just a prank call, but I wasn't going to take any chances. So, I opened my safe, grabbed my K, 9mm, and 12-gauge pistol-grip pump. I already had my 40 cal. because I slept with that by my bed. I will never forget the tone in my wife's voice when she said, "It's 2 a.m. What's going on?" She had this look of concern on her face. I bet she was thinking, *Who have I married — James Bond?* After I explained to her what the person had said on the phone, I told her not to worry because I wasn't going to let anyone do anything to me or her.

If you are wondering why I have all these guns when I say I have changed. The answer is simple: I have changed, but the world that I left has remained the same. Truthfully, it has gotten worse. We don't live in a world that respects people just because they have changed. I also don't believe that guns kill people. I believe people kill people. I believe in obeying the law. The law says I have the right to defend myself, within reasonable limits. So, I'd rather take a chance with having a gun than not having one.

Oh, by the way: Another benefit of taking a chance was that I was able to hire a lawyer and get my record expunged, so all those guns are legit and legal. If I have a choice between whose family is going to have a funeral, someone is going to have to convince me why it should be my family. I was a man — not a thug or hard — just a man. As a man, I wasn't going to run from anything except maybe a dog, snake, and maybe even a mouse. I will run from a man if he has a gun and I don't have one. I realized a long time ago, "One man with a gun can control 100 without one." — Vladimir Lenin. I am one of the 100 if I don't have mine. I am grateful that I am committed not to run from my marriage. It would be wrong for me to say that marriage has been easy. Gail Sheeby said, "To be tested is good. The challenged life may be the best therapist." Yes, marriage is hard, but I am committed to the challenge. I quickly realized it may be okay to run from a mouse, dog, snake, and maybe even a cat, but running from my marriage is not an option. I have enjoyed being married because the institution itself has made me a better man.

I have enjoyed my new life with my wife. Shortly after getting married, we went to Jamaica on a cruise. Have you ever experienced going to sleep to the sound of the ocean crashing against the shore? I have, and I love it! I love looking out the window to a beautiful view of the water from a nice hotel. My wife and I were doing this before we had kids. LOL! Now, I must find a babysitter to keep the closeness in our relationship. We now have three beautiful children — two boys and a girl. I made a commitment to my wife seven years ago, and the plan is to stay faithful and focused on the task. I am no longer daydreaming about being a husband and a father. I am now living this dream.

Mary Tyler Moore said, "Take chances; make mistakes. That's how you grow. Pain nourishes your courage. You have to fail in order to practice being brave."

After you finish reading my story, I know you will realize life is not about getting a chance — it's about *taking* chances. I am encouraging you to take chances because you never know how your life may turn out. The life I am living today is not just for me. It is for anyone who dares to believe.

Naeem Callaway said, "Sometimes the smallest step in the right direction ends up being the biggest step of your life. Tiptoe if you must, but take the step." Here I am, living an entirely different life from the one I was living before. How did that happen? I was willing to take a chance. None of this would have been possible if I had not decided to take a chance.

In Chapter 7, I will show you how I almost put myself in the position to go to prison for the rest of my life because I was so determined to be real.

"Failure of perspective in decision making can be due to aspects of the social utility paradox, but more often results from simple mistakes caused by inadequate thought." —Herman Kahn

7

REAL

Hanging out past midnight was a goal I had when I was 16. In 1990, I was 20 years old and still living at home with my parents. My parents were strict, so that goal wasn't possible to achieve unless I was with my older cousin Teddy. Teddy was what we would call an "O.G." —original gangster. O.G. means someone who has put in work and has earned their respect in the streets. He loved the streets. He stayed in the streets. He always had a car with rims and sounds. He was a hustler with a capital "H" — for real. Teddy had 50 different ways to make money. He was never going to be broke for an extended amount of time.

I was 20 years old, hanging out with my cousin. I loved hanging out with Teddy. Spending time with him gave me some street credentials — "creds." He was well known throughout the city. He wasn't afraid of going to jail, like I was. He spent a lot of time in jail and did more than seven years in prison. While hanging with him, I learned a lot about the streets. My cousin Teddy told me that, if I had a problem with someone, I should never handle my business when my enemy is with his boys. Always wait to catch him by himself. And 10 out of 10 times, he would sing a different song. I took that advice, and it worked. I was hooked with catching people by themselves — which is totally different from the way they do it in the streets today. He also taught me how to behave and act when I am around some real street cats. He told me to never be afraid of anyone. Respect them — yes. Afraid — never! You are as crazy as them. What can they do to you that you can't do to them? He also helped me to overcome some of my fears when hanging out in some crazy spots like 3rd and Potter, Projects, Lapeer Street, and, of course, the car wash on Genesee.

It was late one night, and we were on Genesee St., called the "strip," where everybody hung out. While hanging out at the car wash, Teddy began shooting dice with some O.G.s, and an argument began. I remember him telling me to go to the car and get the gun. It felt so good for me to stand there and watch his back. If anything went down, he would handle the situation, or I would have to shoot someone for the first time.

Either way, we were going to do what we had to do *together* to survive that night. It taught me to survive every night. Being around him made me feel good, because the more people you know, the more respect and love you get on the streets. By hanging out with him, I got to know a lot of older cats from the city.

On this night, the phone rang at 1:00 a.m. It was Teddy. He told me he'd just got jumped and for me to bring my gun. It was nothing for me to jump out of bed and to go and make sure he was alright. For some reason, I went without taking my gun, even though I knew if the guys who jumped my cousin were there, we were going to kill someone. It could have been fear of going to jail; it certainly wasn't fear of killing someone. My cousin was angry, and he didn't play. I made a dumb-but-brave decision and went to meet him without my gun.

When I got there, he told me four men had jumped him and that he'd lost his gold jewelry during the scuffle. We went back to the house where the fight had taken place. With flashlights, we looked around outside for his gold, not knowing if these men were in the house or gone.

Most people would have called the police and let them take care of it. In the streets, that is not how things are done. Situations like this, we handle ourselves. It's called street justice.

The following days and nights, I took it upon myself to look for the dudes who'd jumped my cousin. Every time I rode past the house, I was searching for them. One day I drove my Cadillac past the house where my cousin had been jumped. I was listening to my beat, high as ever, and I saw this dude who didn't like my cousin because of a girl. He jumped off the porch and started running toward my car. Either that girl had told him what kind of car I drove, or word had gotten out that I was looking for the dudes who jumped Teddy.

I slowed down to see what this fool was going to do. To my surprise, he kept coming toward my car. He probably was going to try to do more to me than he'd done to my cousin. So, I pulled off and went home to get my gun. I called my cousin and told him what happened. My cousin laughed and told me to shoot him. There were very few times I would leave the house without my gun. This night I got caught with my pants down. I was slipping.

I am nothing like my cousin. Truthfully, I was soft, trying to be hard. My cousin was the real deal. Don't' forget: The goal for me was to become hard. So, I had to do whatever it took to get that respect from those streets. I got

my gun, wiped off all my bullets, put my gloves on, rolled me a joint and smoked it on my way back to find him. I was about a block from the house. My heart was pounding so loud and hard that it drowned out the music playing in the car. I knew that this was it. I was about to shoot him in his face, and I was going to get out of the car and keep shooting.

I got to the street and slowed down, approaching the house. Nobody was there. I said to myself, *You have got to be kidding me. It's only been about 35 minutes.* I was so amped up and mad because he wasn't there. He was gone.

Looking back on my life then and on my life now, I'm grateful that nobody was on that porch when I drove back over there. I am grateful that I had to go home and get my gun instead of having it on me, like usual. My life could have gone in a different direction if anyone had been outside that house. Then, I began putting myself in situations that would have cost me my freedom and possibly my life.

It wasn't an accident that I left my gun at home and the guys who jumped my cousin weren't there that night or when I drove back to the house. In chapter 8, I will show you how I was as reliable as they come.

J. Donald Walters said, "You will find peace not by trying to escape your problems but by confronting them courageously. You will find peace not in denial, but in victory."

8

RELIABLE

Just another day in the hood, my friend Jaguar got locked up. He asked me to keep his guns for him while he was locked up. I already had three guns of my own — two .38s and a .32. He had a .380 and a brand-new nine. I felt invincible. I had five guns on me, thinking I was the man, not realizing I could have been doing 20 years for having five guns on me in Michigan.

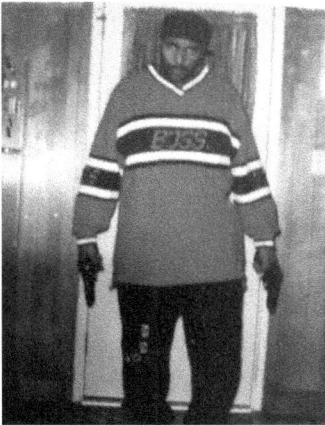

I remember one day going over to my friend Tiger's house. It was in 1994, when I was 24 years old. Tiger asked to see my guns. I gave him the two .38s and he said, in front of everybody, "What are you going to do now that I have your guns?" I remember how good it felt to reach into my pants pull out the .380 and the nine. The whole house went crazy. They were like, "This dude is crazy! How many guns do you have on you?" I said "five," with great pride.

My friend Jaguar ended up getting more time than he thought he would get, so he sent one of his friends, Fly, over to my house for his guns.

Now I didn't know this dude at all — for all I knew, he could have been the police. So, I told him I wasn't giving him any guns. I told him to tell Jaguar I would give him his guns personally when he gets home, and that is exactly what I did. At the time, I guess Jaguar didn't know if he could trust me or not. When Jaguar came home, I returned to him both of his guns. I wanted him to know I was reliable. I could have done like everyone else and lied or come up with some story about how I had to throw his gun, but that wasn't in my nature. Real cats don't steal from their boys.

I was mad because Jaguar should have known he could trust me, and he knew how I was rolling. I didn't like people I didn't know coming to my house.

The guy, Fly, who jaguar had sent to my house, I guess, was supposed to be tough. He was trying to start up this gang, and he took offense to the fact that I would not give him the guns.

So, I started hearing around town that Fly was going to do something to me for not giving him the guns. I said to myself, *He already knows what I have, so all he must do is come and see me.*

Some months passed by and I went to a friend's party. Guess who I saw at the party? You guessed it — Fly and about eight of his homeboys. I wasn't too concerned because there were more than 50 of us in the house, and we were all close. So, I got high and drunk, just having a good time, and as I was sitting at the table, I noticed that one of his little followers was giving me the finger. I was so drunk that, in that moment, I was afraid because I could hardly stand up or see straight.

So, I went and told my friend Snake what had happened and told him to be ready just in case something popped off. He said not to worry about it — that there were too many of us for anyone to think of doing anything to any of us. I always knew that if someone started shooting, there was only so much your friends could do for you at that time. So, I went into the bathroom and took out my gun, the 9-millimeter, and put one in the chamber so that I could be ready to fire at any time. I remember saying in my heart, *I am going to kill one of these dudes tonight if they run up on me. I'm going to shoot everybody and anything that is moving. I'm going to just keep shooting —*

period. I had a 17-shot nine. At the time I wasn't thinking about my family, the families of these guys, the police, jail, or the 100 witnesses who were in the building. All I was thinking about was that my heart was beating like I was in a dark room by myself and I saw something move.

Here I was in this situation where I couldn't leave because people would think that I was scared or that I was a punk. I decided to stay, which put my life and freedom on the line. I stayed until the end of the night. It was 2:00 a.m., and, to my surprise, they never tried anything. But I stayed close to my boys that night, and I escaped another night — because I really was going to kill someone if they ran up on me.

Looking back over my life, I am so grateful they did not test me that night. You better believe Shawn Moore was going to pass the test. Some might believe it was just fate. I don't think so; I was having too many close calls.

In Chapter 9, I will show you how ridiculous I had started behaving.

"One stupid mistake can change everything." — Picturequotes.com

9

RIDICULOUS

I bought my first gun in 1987, at the age of 17. It was a nine-shot .22 that I bought from one of my cousin Teddy's friends. It was the gun I used in my first and only drive-by. I don't remember that entire incident, but I do remember somebody had done something disrespectful to one of my friends. So, we got high and drove by the guy's house, got out of the car, and took turns shooting at the house.

I remember being so afraid of getting caught and going to jail for shooting up a house with a .22 — not even knowing who was in the house. I was so relieved to watch and hear on the news that no one had been shot. I never told my friends how I really felt. At the time I was shooting, I just didn't care, because I had to let my friends know that I was down for whatever. How ridiculous it is to shoot into a house without knowing who was inside or where people were in the house! Tony Robbins said, "It is in your moments of decision that your destiny is shaped." Boy, was that true with the decisions I was making in my life.

That same .22 was with me the night I went up to a local school in my neighborhood, and this rival gang just happened to be outside on the sidewalk. There were more than 100 of them just standing there looking at me and three of my friends in a Pontiac 1000. They knew exactly who we were. We lived in a small town, and I was always hanging out, and, with this new gun on me, I was itching to use it.

Once again, in the streets, the more work you put in, the more respect you get. So, I know I had to be willing to put in work because I was craving respect.

So, we were sitting in the car looking at them, and they were looking at us. We were stuck in traffic because the parking lot was jam-packed. Suddenly traffic started moving.

This was on a Friday night at a game at a local middle school. When we went back to school Monday, one of the guys who was related to one of the gang members told me we were lucky we pulled off when we did because they were going to bum rush my car. I told him I'm glad they didn't bum rush my car because I would have shot somebody. Period! I must say that life in the streets is not fair. The streets will force you to do things you might not want to do. Deep down inside, I didn't want to shoot anyone, but I couldn't allow myself to be scared to come outside or to go certain places. Who is going to respect you when you are afraid to go places out of fear of being shot or jumped? I always felt like I was a cool dude, but I had to watch my back just because of what side of town I lived on. You tell me: How is that fair?

I don't believe I was just fortunate that they did not bum rush my car and force me to shoot someone. In Chapter 10, I will show you how close I was to going to jail for a very long time.

"Is it possible to have several close calls, come out on the winning side, and say there is no God?" — Shawn Moore

10

CLOSE

One of my friends, Cheetah, was just like me. In 1993, I was 23 years old. Cheetah always had a gun on him. He was a little worse, because he'd been put in a few situation where he had to use his guns, and because of that, he had clout in the streets. Cheetah and I were talking. He was so happy that he had four guns. He'd gone to a party with three of our friends — Python, Lion, and Worm — and he could give all three of them a gun. They were all strapped with his guns — a .44, a .357, .38, and a .22. The .44 had a 7.5-inch barrel, like Clint Eastwood used to carry in his *Dirty Harry* movies. At the time, I only had a little .380 and a .38. My friend Cheetah would let certain people in the hood hold a gun from time to time — especially those he knew wouldn't come back with a made-up story about why they had to throw the gun and they didn't have it anymore.

He knew I wasn't like that. I was loyal, true, trustworthy, and not a liar. I had the privilege of keeping the .44 on several occasions. This day I was coming home from picking up my daughter. At the time, she was only about 13 months old. As I was riding past a store on

Genessee St., one of the guys I went to school with who was related to one of the gang members who didn't like me because of the neighborhood I grew up in, threw his hands in the air to me, like saying, "What's up?"

I didn't know what he wanted or what his real intentions were. The store he was at was one where people were getting jumped and shot all the time. So, no way was I going to stop up there with my baby in the car. I put my finger out the window as if to say, "I will be back in one minute...give me a minute." I floored it home, got the .44, and dropped my baby off to my mom's. The humor in this story is that I ended up taking care of this baby for five years. I lost my job, and the mother demanded I take a blood test, trying to get child support from me. I fell behind, but I came to find out the baby wasn't mine. My family was devastated. I know I was wrong, but all I could think about was saving some money. My parents still have her pictures up in their home today. We loved that baby, but here I was leaving the baby with my mom to see what this guy wanted with me. I went around the corner to pick up one of my boys to go with me. Python told me "No," but Lion came with me.

Lion and I went back up to the store, and my man was gone. I told Lion, "Let's ride by his house." So, we did, and when we got there, he had at least 30 people in the yard with him. So, we just rode past, real slow, just letting him know that, if he wanted some trouble, I wasn't hiding. Truthfully, I was foolish because we only had six shots with that .44 and the odds were that, out of the 30, at least six of them were strapped. I quickly took Lion home and thanked him for coming with me.

A few months went by. Cheetah and I were hanging out and guess what we had with us? You're right — the .44. And we're drunk and high, having a good time. Cheetah said he was hungry, and we decided to go to Bridgeport to get something to eat. Bridgeport was the good side of town, so you know where this story is going. We made the decision to drop the .44 off at home and then go get something to eat.

It was about 2:00 a.m. As we were driving to get something to eat, the State Police pulled us over and asked to search the truck. As they were searching, they found some .44 bullets and asked where the 44 was.

Cheetah told him it was his brother's gun. He probably had it at home. Fifteen minutes earlier, we'd had that gun in the truck with us already for several hours — we both had enemies. So, having a gun guaranteed some protection. I don't think it's a coincidence that we were that close to being caught with that gun.

A former president said that learning to stand in somebody else's shoes, to see through their eyes, that's how peace begins. And it's up to you to make that happen. Empathy is a quality of character that can change the world. I can't help but feel the pain of all those who are locked up or headed in that direction when I have had so many close calls.

In Chapter 11, I will show you how my hanging out with my friends landed me in jail.

"When someone makes a decision, he is really diving into a strong current that will carry him to places he had never dreamed of when he first made the decision." — Paul Coelho

11

FRIENDS

Nothing felt better than knowing that someone we were close to was having a party. In 1990, I was 20 years old. This was one of those nights, and I couldn't wait. I always felt safe at these parties because I knew the odds were in our favor and I could relax and enjoy my buzz.

This was a house party hosted by Cheetah's cousin, and everybody was there: Snake, Anaconda, Worm, Tiger, Crocodile, Cat, Python, Lion, and many others. Everyone was having a good time. It was around 12:30 a.m., and Tiger had done something to offend Donkey and Monkey. They were going to fight him, not knowing that Tiger was with us. All of a sudden, I heard the words, "It's going down," and next thing I know, we were all fighting just Donkey and Monkey. There was no way they could beat all of us. So there really was no need for what happened next.

Python, who is the real deal, pulls out the .44 that Cheetah would let us carry from time to time and started pistol-whipping Donkey. I will never forget the sound of that gun going up against the head of Donkey again and again and all the blood that was flowing from his head. I remember hearing screams from many different people and seeing people running everywhere.

You guessed it — the party was over. So, I quickly ran to my car, and Worm came with me, while everyone else went their separate ways. All we could hear were sirens. When I turned the corner, I could see nothing but lights — and then I saw the police hit a U-turn. I knew they were going to pull us over. I wasn't too concerned because, in my mind, we weren't the ones who'd pistol whipped anyone, and I did not have the .44. But I did have my dad's .32.

When I made the decision to carry my dad's gun for protection, at first it seemed like a good idea. Then I realized that decision was probably going to land me in jail. My dad kept his .32 in his dresser drawer, and, for years, I had been sneaking it out and carrying it for protection. My dad never knew I was stealing his gun. He thought it didn't work. So, when they called him and told him, "Mr. Moore, we have your son," he told them that they were mistaken. They asked him to go check his drawer, and he did. To his surprise, he had to admit and actually say the words, "Yes, you have my son, and my gun is missing.

When they pulled Worm and me over, the .32 was under Worm's seat, but I told them it was my gun, which it was. I had never been arrested before and really wasn't trying to get arrested. This was going to be my first time going to jail. Anyone who knows me knows that I am a picky eater and that I love to eat. It did not take me long to realize that jail was not for me. Life in jail isn't fair. You need to know someone to have favor. Three people left and a new guy came in. But because he knew somebody who was already there, he got one of the beds that were available, even though I and some others were next in line to get beds. It was then that I knew jail wasn't for me. I did not want to add another charge for fighting for a bed, so I just chilled and thought to myself, *This mess is crazy.*

I had to sleep on the floor due to over-crowdedness, and I traded my trays of food for chips, so I was hungry. The only comfort for me was that Worm and Tiger were in the cell with me, and a few more of my friends were locked up as well. I remember Tiger's parents coming to get him, and then Worm's parents came. I called my parents, crying and begging for them not to leave me there. After three days, my parents finally came and got me, and I thought I had learned my lesson. It was then I knew jail wasn't for me. Because I couldn't have my gun in jail, and sleeping on the floor due to over-crowdedness wasn't cool.

Now this is the part of the story that doesn't make sense. I didn't want to be locked up. I didn't like being locked up, but I didn't change my lifestyle. I started doing even *more* wrong. I kept hanging around the same people and doing the same things even after I got out of jail. The decisions I was making could have landed me in jail for a long time. I started selling more drugs and carrying more guns after I was sentenced to probation for attempted CCW with the plea. I wish I could say them giving me a second chance helped me, but it didn't. I only got worse.

It wasn't mere coincidence that I went to jail only one more time in my life, for about three hours for having some weed.

I heard someone say "Don't lose hope. You never know what tomorrow will bring." In Chapter 12, I will show you how having a little glimpse of hope paid off for me.

"Good things come to those who wait...better things come to those who don't give up...and the best things come to those who believe!" — Unknown

12

HOPE

In 1998, I was 28 years old, and, deep down inside, I knew I could do more with my life than what I was doing. I had no real assets, and my future seemed hopeless. I was angry, depressed, confused, and lost, and I had no life- changing goals. I said to myself, *If I am ever going to change, the time is now.*

So, I decided to stop selling — and using — drugs. I decided to stop hanging around my friends all the time, like I used to. I wasn't going to be involved in any illegal activities anymore. This was a hard decision, because I loved having money and things. The only thing I loved more than money was my freedom. I felt in my heart that, if I didn't change, I was going to end up dead or locked up. So, I took a chance and decided to try to change.

Someone said, "Difficult roads often lead to beautiful destinations." That statement is so true in my life. In 2006, it had been eight years since I decided to change. The journey had been very difficult because I have had to learn how to manage my money like never before.

If I didn't want to be broke, I needed to learn how to manage my money, because I could not just go hustle or make moves that would bring in some income anymore. Living check to check was one of the greatest lessons I have had to learn through this whole decision to change. Learning to be content and knowing the value of bargain shopping are both priceless bits of knowledge to have.

Someone asked me, "What's your favorite childhood memory?" Answer: Not paying Bills. Someone else said, "There's no way a person was born to just pay bills and die." I could relate to these statements. In 2006, I had only enough money to pay the bills, and I remember crying out to God about how unfair life was. Here I was, trying to live right, trying to do the right thing, and it seems that people who weren't living right had way more than I did.

I am inclined to agree with Celestine Chua: "Success is 99% attitude and 1% aptitude." I really wasn't doing all that bad. I had two cars, an old Caprice and a minivan. All my bills were paid. I lived on the good side of town, with no roommates, like I had previously, in college. I wasn't starving. I just didn't have a lot of money to buy things I didn't really need but just wanted.

After I was done crying about my life, I took time just to reflect on how good my life really was compared to where I was headed before I decided to change. I wasn't locked up. I had been sober for eight years, and my future was bright. So, I decided to live a life of gratitude instead of complaining.

It wasn't long after I changed my attitude that I received a raise and a promotion. I learned a valuable lesson: Just because something isn't happening for you right now doesn't mean that it will never happen. *You can't quit.* Eventually you will reap what you sow. Success has no time limit. You will never be a successful person overnight. It takes time. I am so glad I did not give up even though I wanted to so many times.

Leo Rosten said, "Money can't buy happiness, but neither can poverty." Please don't misunderstand what I am about to share with you. Because of the raise, I went from barely making it to being able to save more than $1,000 a month, with much money to spare.

I could give away money if someone needed something. I was able to pay for people's meals when we went out to eat. I bought a new car. I bought lots of guns. I moved from my apartment to purchasing my first home. I sold the Caprice and van and paid cash for an old-school 1978 Oldsmobile 98. I went to the store and paid cash for my rims. I remember looking at my bank statement. I had a little more than $10,000 in my account!

My life was good not because of the money or prosperity but because I knew then that I had made the right decision in 1998 to change my life. James Belasco and Ralph Stayer said, "Change is hard because people overestimate the value of what they have and underestimate the value of what they may gain by giving that up."

I am a happy man right now because what I have gained and the man I have become have far exceeded my expectations of what I had hoped for in my decision to change. As you continue to read my story, I know you will see that I made the right decision to change.

In Chapter 13, I will show you how outrageous my thinking had started to be.

"Your real friends will always have your back, no matter how badly things may go." — Unknown

13

OUTRAGEOUS

In 1993, I was 23 years old. One of my favorite things to do was sitting at my friend's house, smoking weed, with drugs in my pocket, guns nearby, and hanging out. I remember one day looking around the room and seeing a bunch of thugs and killers. I said to myself, *Nobody better mess with us right now.* It was a good feeling to have that kind of power and security to know that if something went down, we could and would take care of business.

One of my fondest memories is when I saw my friend Panther on Genessee Street on the corner of Weber. So, I pulled into the parking lot to talk to him, and another car pulled up. All I saw was Panther's hand come out the window, with his 9millimeter pointed at the guy in the car. The guy pulled off, and Panther started to chase him. I remember laughing and saying that Panther was crazy. People used to mess with him because of his small stature, but, in the streets, size doesn't matter — especially when you have a gun. I was grateful that he was my friend and not my enemy.

In the late '80s, gangs were a big problem in Saginaw. My neighborhood was a small gang but was connected to every other gang in Saginaw. All of us knew somebody in the other gangs who were cool, or we were related somehow. It's crazy when you really think about what I just said. I remember buying my first sawed-off shot gun from one of my boys who was in one of these other gangs we were connected to. The more guns I accumulated, the safer I felt hanging around these guys. I felt like I was accepted by my friends, and I needed that kind of acceptance at the time.

Nothing was better than being in a room with a bunch of crazy cats just like me — to feel like I was welcome somewhere and that someone loved me. I could do whatever and be whatever and say whatever, and people still respected and loved me just the way I was.

This night, we were doing what we do — sitting around with a house full of women and smoking weed. I had just bought a new gun — one of the biggest .38s available. It was nice and fat and bigger than some .357s. I needed to go to the store and get some more blunts, but I was too high to take the gun with me. so I left it with two of my friends, Jaguar and Cheetah. Being so high, I knew that, if I got pulled over, I would be searched. When we walked outside, I noticed three or four guys hanging outside about six houses down on the opposite side of the street. I didn't think much of it, so I left and went to the store alone.

When I came back, Jaguar handed me my gun empty. I came to find out that those guys we'd noticed were from a rival gang. They'd had a shootout while I was gone, and Jaguar had used my gun. I thought to myself, *Every time something happens, I'm either at work, just leaving, or just pulling up.* I was so upset because I needed to earn stripes, and to earn stripes, you must put in work. So I was disappointed because I wasn't involved in the shooting activities that my friends were so randomly and actively involved in.

I don't believe I was just fortunate to be at the store at the time of the shootout, do you? In Chapter 14, I will show you how loyal I was.

"That awkward moment when you think you're important to someone, and you're not." — *quote.snydle.com*

14

LOYAL

In 1995, I was 25 years old. This night, I was with my friend Cat, and we decided to go over to this girl's house that he had been dating. When we walked into the house, we noticed the house was full. There were nine gang members, some related to the girl Cat was dating, and we went to school with about four of them, so we didn't think there was going to be any problems. I quickly noticed they were all mostly drunk and that they were smoking weed. So, we joined them in getting high, and one of them asked me where my gun was and what kind I had. At the time, I didn't think it was a strange question. I thought they were just trying to have conversation.

I told them that I had a .38 and that I had left it in my car. So now they knew I didn't have my gun on me. About four of them went outside, two of whom I knew from school, and I remember my car alarm went off, so I ran to the door. But they said one of them had bumped my car and that the alarm had gone off. At the time, I had no reason to doubt the story. But on the following day, I realized that someone had keyed my car, and it had to be one of them.

So, we were getting high, and I overheard them talking about doing something to somebody. Cat and I were the only people in the house not in their clique. So, I went into the living room, where Cat was with this girl, to tell him what I'd heard. Cat was a wild and strong dude. He was always ready for a fight, and he knew how to fight. We decided that night that Cat was going to be Booker T and I was Stevie Ray (better known as Harlem Heat).

At the private school, I had been in quite a few fights and had gotten pretty good with my hands, so I wasn't afraid, even though it was nine of them and only two of us. So, I took off all my gold rings and started to hide my jewelry when all of them started to come into the living room with us. At the time, I was standing next to Cat, but I moved close to the door so we could spread the floor. One thing we thought was in our favor was that they were drunk — sloppy drunk — and we hadn't drunk a thing.

While I was standing at the door, five or six of them surrounded Cat, and one of them pulled out a nine-millimeter and was pushing Cat's head with his finger and they were talking big junk about him messing with the girl he was dating. I guess she was dating one of them as well.

The plan was that I would take four or five of them, and he would handle the rest, but they had surrounded him. One of them we had gone to school with looked at me and said "Bear," which was my street name, "you can leave. We only have a problem with Cat." Although I will always have mad love and respect for him giving me the opportunity to leave, I looked him in the face and told him that I wasn't leaving Cat there with them. I guess my man didn't realize how far Cat and I went back. Cat was the one who gave me my street name. One day over at Python and Lion's house, we were getting high, and I grabbed Cat and held him tight. He said, "Get off me, you big bear." It went from a joke to who I was. I tried to live as if I really were a bear. Have you ever seen anyone running up on a bear without a gun? Not a wise decision. So, it was nothing for me to say that we'd come here together and that we were leaving together.

At that moment, I made eye contact with Cat, and I could see it in his eyes that he was about to rush the one with the gun, which wasn't a good idea, so I shook my head side to side, saying, "No." I am glad he listened to me because all they did was threaten him and push his head with their finger. Cat was a crazy dude and if he would have done what he wanted to do, who knows what the outcome would have been for us? After they warned him, they ran through the house yelling and screaming not to mess with them, and then they left.

I remember being so mad when we left that house! I was thinking that, when we get back to the hood, it was on. But a good part of my crew didn't want any trouble because we went to school with these guys. Only a few of my friends were ready to ride, and most of them were not my friends from the neighborhood, which hurt me bad because I thought we were like family. Sometimes we expect more from others because we would be willing to do that much for them. I learned a valuable lesson that night. If something really had gone down, I had to be prepared to do my dirt by myself if I had to.

I don't believe it's a coincidence that I walked out of that house alive that night, do you? Or that no one in my immediate crew wanted to do anything about the incident? In Chapter 15, I will show you how I was betrayed.********

"Everyone suffers at least one bad betrayal in their lifetime. It's what unites us. The trick is not to let it destroy your trust in others when that happens. Don't let them take that from you."

— SHERRILYN KENYON

15

BETRAYAL

The saddest thing about betrayal is that it doesn't come from your enemies but from those close to you. I was 26 years old and looking forward to hanging out with my good friend Snake. Snake was my guy. Someone had broken into my family's shed and stolen our lawnmower. Snake was right there with my dad and me, chasing the man around our neighborhood and getting our lawnmower back. Snake rode to school with me every day. Whenever I had problems in the streets, Snake was one of the few people I could count on to have my back. He was always ready for whatever. He had my back regardless of how many or who it was. My enemies were his enemies, and vice versa. Whenever Snake would hook up with a girl, he would hook me up with her friend. Real talk: It would take an entire different book to tell you all that Snake and I have been through together. Truthfully, most of it I, would refuse to talk about.

On this day, I arrived at Snake's house in the evening; Cat was there as well. Snake told me he wanted to drive, which was odd. Whenever Snake and I hung out, I was always the one behind the wheel. Then, Snake said something even more strange: He asked me not to bring my gun! I had never heard him make such a request in my life! Snake had more people that didn't like him than I did. At the time, I was wearing more than $3,000 in gold jewelry. I had dope and a lot of money on me, and I didn't care for the idea of not having my gun on me. Snake and I argued about this for 15 minutes, and I finally gave in to him. He said he didn't feel right having the gun in the car. I said, "Okay — if that's how you feel, I'll leave my gun at home."

We were headed to a nightclub, and Snake said that he needed to make a stop first. We went to a strange neighborhood, and I didn't feel safe at all. I started asking questions about who lived there, how long were we going to be there, and what were we doing there in the first place? Snake tried to reassure me and stated that we wouldn't be long at all. We were just sitting at this strange house, for apparently no reason. Snake said that he was meeting someone, and I got mad. I kept thinking, *I shouldn't have listened to Snake. I should have brought my gun.* We just sat there for about 30 minutes. We rolled up a joint in the time that we were waiting, but I really couldn't enjoy getting high, not knowing where we were. I could tell Snake was in no hurry to leave, but we did finally leave.

C.S. Lewis once said that we laugh at honor and are shocked to find traitors in our midst. Snake, Cat, and I finally made it to the club and had a good time. We left the club about 1:00 a.m., and I was ready to go. As we are driving home, my pager went off; it was Cobra. I asked Snake to pull over so I could use a pay phone. While on the phone, Gorilla pulled up and jumped out of his car with a .357 magnum and was standing about ten feet away from me. I had no idea what to do since I didn't have a gun on me. As Gorilla was coming toward me, I told Cobra what was happening and to call the police. Then I just stayed on the phone as if I were still talking, and Gorilla just stood there, staring at me.

Cat jumped out of the car and tried to talk to Gorilla. Then another car pulled up. In this third car was one of our home girls from the neighborhood. I hung up the phone and went over to her car to give her my jewelry, my money, and the drugs I had in my pocket. I told her to leave and that I would call her later to get my stuff. Then I got into the car with Snake and asked him why he was just sitting there and not talking to Gorilla, since he had made me leave my gun at home. He couldn't respond, because the parking lot was swarming with police by then.

Gorilla took off running, and the police didn't even bother to chase him. They questioned Snake, Cat, and me because, when Cobra called the police, he told them someone was being robbed, and they automatically assumed it was the store. When they realized it was just us in the parking lot and that there was nothing happening in the store, you could see them quickly lose interest in the situation.

After the police left, the three of us drove back to the hood so that I could get my stuff from our home girl, but what I really wanted was to get my gun. Our girl met us at Snake's house, and, while we were telling her what had happened, the phone rang. It was Gorilla. I wasn't that surprised that he had not been caught by the police.

Snake was talking to him, but I took the phone and told Gorilla that I hoped he was ready to do what he had to when the time came. I was letting him know he'd better be ready to shoot if he was going to be messing around with me. Gorilla said he was and that he didn't care. I asked him why he hadn't done anything except stand there staring at me. His response almost floored me. Gorilla said he hadn't done anything because he wasn't sure that Snake had kept his end of the deal by making sure I didn't have a gun on me. I didn't want to believe Gorilla, but I knew it was true, because Snake had never asked me to leave my gun behind before. I don't know why Snake was setting me up, and I never asked him about it. In fact, I never told him I knew about it. I just handed the phone back to Snake and never said a word about it. I was once again reminded that I couldn't trust anyone — not even someone I thought was a good friend. I was also thinking I needed to get more guns. Vin Diesel said, "I always have issues with trust." With this happening to me, I was faced with the reality that I really couldn't trust anyone.

Martin Luther King, Jr. once said that he had decided to stick to love because hate is too great a burden to bear. When I was in the streets, there was one rapper that I listened to more than anyone else — Tupac. Tupac had said, "Keep your enemies close, and watch your homies." There was no way I was going to push Snake out of my life. I kept him close until the day he died. Only a few of my homies knew what he'd tried to do to me, but I never treated him differently. However, from that point on, I always drove.

Snake played a big part in why I was carrying more than one gun. Every time I bought a new gun, I would go straight to his house and show it to him. He would say that I was crazy and would ask me what was going on. I would tell him I didn't know who I could trust and that I wasn't going to let anyone take my life. As much as I wanted to believe that statement, I have heard of and know of some real street cats who have died from being shot. The truth of the matter is that no one is in control of when they die. When it's your time, it's your time. However, it's humbling to know that your life can be over quick because a gun was in the hands of someone who was not mature and responsible enough to have one. This is not the way the creator designed for us to die.

Nelson Mandela once said, "No one is born hating another person because of the color of his skin, or his background, or his religion. People must *learn* to hate, and if they can learn to hate, they can be *taught* to love, for love comes more naturally to the human heart than its opposite." A lack of love is one of the biggest problems in our streets and in the world today. We have so many young people in jail today for killing people before they assess a situation. Yes, it is a challenge to love someone who has betrayed you. I can tell you from experience that, while it's hard, it *is* possible. Life was going to be hard for me — whatever choice I made. I decided to take the path of love and forgiveness. I never found out why Snake betrayed me. To me it really didn't matter — he was my boy for life. I just knew I couldn't trust him.

Having a friend like Snake taught me what Scarface said: "Who do I trust? Me! That's who!" For real. However, over my years of being sober I have learned that I can't even trust myself. Sometimes I find myself doing things I don't want to do and the things I should do I can't find the strength to do. So, for me, I have learned the only person I can truly trust is God!

It's not a coincidence that I wasn't shot or robbed — or worse — the night Snake betrayed me. In chapter 16, I will show you how I was protected from harm.

"Power is no blessing except when it is used to protect the innocent."

— Jonathan Swift

16

PROTECTED

"Challenges make life interesting. Overcoming challenges makes life meaningful," said Joshua J. Marine. When I was 18 years old, a car pulled up beside me as I was arriving at school one morning. The driver asked if I was Shawn Moore. I said, "Yes," and he just drove away. That made me nervous and afraid of what was about to happen that day. There was a lot of gang activity during that time, and people were getting shot frequently.

I did some detective work by using what car he was driving to find out who he was. So, I decided to confront him and find out if there was a problem. He accused me of talking about his sister, but I had no idea what he was talking about, as I didn't really know his sister or anything about her. I thought everything was cool after I talked to him, but I wasn't sure.

Later that night, I was hanging out on Genessee Street. This was known as "The Strip" in Saginaw and was about a mile or two long. Every weekend we would park in the lots of the local businesses up and down the street. The street would be packed with cars driving back and forth all along The Strip. It was the place to see and be seen.

My cousin Teddy loved Genessee Street. If I wanted to find him, I just had to drive The Strip, and, eventually, I'd run into him. Some friends of mine, Snake, Buffalo, and Wolf, along with five others and myself were hanging with Teddy in the parking lot across from the car wash. The same dude I had confronted earlier in the day pulled up and jumped out of the car with three of his friends. I had already told my cousin and friends what had happened that morning, and it turned out that Teddy knew the guy. Teddy ran up on him, and they talked. When they finished, the dude came over to me, gave me a hug, and we talked. I told him again it was a misunderstanding, since I didn't know his sister. He turned out to be a cool dude, and we have remained cordial toward each other to this day.

That night on The Strip, I wasn't too worried about the situation, since we were about ten deep, including Snake, Wolf, and Buffalo. I remember the first time I met Wolf, which was at the private school I had attended. Wolf was involved in the streets from a young age, and the leaders of this school were trying to help him by finding sponsors to pay tuition for him to attend the private school. Wolf had killers in his family, and he wasn't far from becoming one himself.

Wolf told the leaders at the school that he had enemies, but I don't think they initially believed him. That changed after they sent him out into the neighborhood to invite people to church. He came back with bullet holes in the car and the window shot out. Wolf was the real deal. His family was in and out of jail. Since there weren't too many blacks at the private school, he and I connected and became good friends.

While at the school, some thought that he was taking my lunch from me, but, I was sharing it with Wolf, even though he aggressively asked me for some of my lunch. My parents always blessed me with more food in my lunch than I could eat, so I shared it with Wolf. During that time, Wolf knew that I didn't know a lot about the streets, so he was willing to protect me at school. Wolf wasn't going to let anyone do anything to me, and that made me feel strong and protected. At the time, I was shy, and I had a fear of street people, but having Wolf around helped me lose that fear because I knew he had my back.

Buffalo and I had also met at the same private school, and he was the real deal, just like Wolf. Having a crew that included Wolf and Buffalo made me feel as if I were a part of something. We watched out for each other. For example, we were all three in Bay City, which is predominantly a white area, and we were not welcome. Wolf was having problems with a guy over some girls. It was nothing for me to tell that guy and his friends not to make me pop my trunk. See, in Bay City, black men got pulled over all the time, so I kept my guns in the trunk. When I said that, they just left. To this day, Wolf reminds me about that incident and what I did for him, but it was like that in the streets. One day someone has your back, and, the next day, you would have theirs.

So, that night on The Strip, I knew that Snake, Buffalo, and Wolf would have my back as well as my cousin Teddy and my other friends. Even so, it was not simply luck or a coincidence that Teddy knew that dude and was able to quash it before it came to me. In Chapter 17, I will show you how someone in my family almost got me into some trouble.

"The most important thing in the world is family and love." — John Wooden

17

FAMILY

I was 20 years old and had been working second shift at Arby's, getting off between 11 and 12 at night. One day I was trying to sleep in when the phone rang. It was my little sister, and she was whispering. I knew she was at school, so I wondered what was up. She was in the twelfth grade now only 17 years old. She told me this guy said he was going to slap her because of our cousin, who was affiliated with a gang that he had issues with. I guess he didn't realize how much I loved my family, especially my little sister. I jumped out of bed, got dressed, and drove to my old high school, where she met me at the door. We went to this guy's class and knocked on the door. I was just going to let him know not to threaten my sister when I felt a hand on my shoulder and heard a voice say, "You don't want to do that." It was the school principal, who was one of my teachers when I attended there.

He escorted us to his office, where I explained the situation. He said it was best for me to let him handle it. I left, but I went to get Snake and Cat. We came back to the school around lunchtime and drove through the parking lot to let the guy know I was there. Everyone who was outside saw us, and I was truthfully just trying to scare him. I knew I couldn't really do anything while he was at school without landing in jail. Gossip spreads quickly; besides, the principal had probably spoken to him. I also wanted him to know I was not going to take anyone threatening my little sister and not do anything about it.

About a week later, I saw him riding on Genessee Street. Snake was with me, and I hit a U-turn to pull up beside him. I looked him directly in the eyes and asked him if he wanted to see me. He looked at me and said "No." He could tell that I wasn't playing about my little sister. His response made me feel good that he had enough respect (or fear) for me and my reputation that he didn't want any trouble. Sure, he was only one person and just a kid still in school, and I knew that we still had a lot of work to do to earn our respect from the entire city, but I still felt good.

When I got home that night, my sister was on the phone with a friend of mine who lived around the corner from us. He told her to tell me that there was this guy at his house who said he didn't like me. Without thinking, I got in my car and drove around the corner to my friend's place to check this guy as well. I was feeling pretty good about myself at this point. When I got there, this guy came outside and said, "Nobody messing with you, man. You probably got a gun on you." I looked at him and told him I did — but it turned out that *he* was the one saying he didn't like me. Now, at this point, I was being foolish. This guy could have shot me. If he had just started shooting, there wasn't really anything I could have done about it because I didn't have my finger on the trigger. As far as I knew, he didn't have a gun. But the point I'm trying to make is that he could have had a gun. All I was thinking was that I had to go check this guy because he said he didn't like me. He had tried me a few times throughout the years, so I don't think he was afraid of me. Probably the only thing that saved me on this night was that he knew I most likely had a gun on me. What he didn't know is whether I would use it. My man and I are cordial to this day.

It was not luck or a coincidence that I didn't get myself killed running up on people, trying to earn respect in the streets. I used the same tactics on many other people, and it worked all the time. Most of them wouldn't try to be hard if caught alone, without their homies. People like to act harder than they really are when there is a crowd around. I didn't give people that chance. I was into one on one or that face-to-face business with those who didn't like me. If there was a problem, I was trying to resolve it as quickly as possible, before it escalated. My life was about making money — not killing people. However, I was willing to do it if I had to.

In Chapter 18, I will show you how foolish I had become with carrying a gun.

"I'm sure there are close calls that we're not even aware of hundreds of times a year. You cross the street, and if you'd crossed the street two minutes later, you'd have been hit by a car, but you'd never know it. I'm sure that kind of stuff happens all the time."
— Seth MacFarlane

18

FOOLISH

At the private school I attended, black kids were always coming and going. I was one of the few who attended consistently for years. I went there for about eight years, all the way to the twelfth grade, when I got myself kicked out. Alligator was one of the young black kids who attended for a little while. We were good friends until he moved away and I lost contact with him. Before I tell you about Alligator, I must tell you about Cheetah.

Cheetah and I were hanging out on Bay Road at Stardust, which was a bowling alley and bar. It was risky hanging on Bay Road because the police in that area did not play. Everyone knew you could go to jail in a hurry hanging out there, and it's still that way to this day.

Both Cheetah and I carried guns, and Cheetah was well known and respected. We're having a good time doing what we do — playing pool and spending time with the ladies. We were both high and drunk, and the place was about to close. As we were leaving the parking lot, the police pulled us over. My heart was racing because I had drugs on me, and we both had guns on us. I was so drunk and high that I couldn't walk without staggering.

I asked the officer what was going on, and he said that they were looking for some guy who'd been involved in a fight and he had the same name as "Cheetah." The officer took our IDs and ran the license plates. When he came back to the car, he told us to drive safe, because my friend "Cheetah" was not who he was looking for. I was shocked! He didn't ask to search the vehicle, and he had to know we were drunk and/or high, and yet, he didn't do anything. I just knew we were both going to jail — but it didn't happen!

Now keep that incident in mind while I tell you about Alligator. After losing contact with Alligator for several years, we got back in touch. His sister and mine somehow ended up talking to each other, which allowed Alligator and I to reconnect. He was living in Seattle, Washington, but was returning to Saginaw to visit his dad, who still lived in the area. We got together, and I learned that Alligator also smoked weed. We left to go get some and got high. His cousin came over, and we went for a ride. While we were out riding around, the police pulled up behind us. There was smoke coming out the windows of the car, but we quickly put out the joint. We figured we were about to be pulled over. Everyone knew that if more than two black men were in the car, the possibility of getting pulled over rose dramatically. I also had a gun on me, and I just knew that we were going to jail. The car smelled like weed, and, if the police had pulled us over, he would have gotten a contact high as soon as he got out of his patrol car. To my surprise, the officer followed us for about three miles but never pulled us over. I think he just wanted to make us sweat. Well the plan worked. I was wet, and my heart was pounding as hard as if I'd been in the ocean and seen a shark fin.

We headed to Tiger's house to continue smoking weed. Now Tiger's house was the place to be. Not only was it permissible to smoke weed there, but people came to Tiger's house all through the day and night. I wanted to show Alligator and his cousin a good time, and Tiger's house was the place to hang out because women were always over there.

One of my friends, Crocodile, was also at Tiger's, and he was being disrespectful. I can't remember exactly what he said, but it was inappropriate for the time. I hadn't seen Alligator in years, and I couldn't let him think I was a punk by letting Crocodile disrespect me like that. So, I hit Crocodile in the mouth and told him to shut up. I sucker-punched him in front of a house full of people. I was so determined to get my respect that I acted without thinking. But honestly, I didn't do that to everyone who I felt disrespected me.

In other cases, I let it pass because I knew that I would have to kill some dudes, as there wouldn't be any fighting — at least not hand-to-hand combat fighting. I remember having a bad temper and problems controlling my anger. I can remember when my thoughts progressed from beating up people to killing them. I would visualize myself killing someone by shooting them directly in the face multiple times. I would see myself standing over them and emptying the clip into their body. I would think about killing their entire family. I thought I was losing my mind because I had such messed-up thoughts.

I am thankful that Crocodile didn't challenge me that day because I did have a gun on me. Hitting him like that broke one of the personal rules I had for myself. That rule was that I was no longer going to fight or put my hands on anyone. I viewed it as a waste of time to beat someone up, because that would give them a reason to go get their friends and family and then come back with a gun. My philosophy was to talk it out, to reconcile, and to seek peace. The only other alternative was to start with the guns. Instead of talking to Crocodile, I let my emotions get the best of me, and I hit him. Thankfully, he didn't let his emotions get the best of him and let it pass. Then — and now — there is (usually) no forgiveness in the streets.

Three different scenarios and each time, I was able to walk away without going to jail or getting shot. It was not a coincidence. I told you about the story with Cheetah first so you can see how foolishly I was living — yet I wasn't getting caught like everyone else. At the time I didn't understand it. I thought I was just lucky or street smart. But in the final chapter, I am going to share with you what I believe was going on.

In Chapter 19, I will show you how insane my life was becoming.

"It is in your moments of decision that your destiny is shaped." — Tony Robbins

19

INSANE

My relationship with my girlfriend of nine years was going bad. I still had my girlfriend of seven years, but it still hurt knowing that my first relationship was coming to an end. Now, pay attention to my insane way of thinking. I always told my old girlfriend not to disrespect me. The rule was not to cheat on me. I didn't want guys, in the streets, laughing at me because they were sleeping with my girl. Remember, I had already forgiven her for what I told you she'd done in Chapter 4. If she didn't respect me enough to remain loyal it would be hard for people in the streets to respect you if your woman did not. I was serious about my women being loyal to Shawn Moore! Honestly, when I say "women," I had more friends than just these two, but those relationships were open.

When my old girlfriend started going out in public with some guy I did not know for the first time. I took it as she was being very disrespectful too soon. It was difficult especially since my friends were coming back and telling me they saw her out.

Yes, officially, we were no longer a couple. However, that had happened many times before — but we always got back together. I would have been okay with moving on with my new girlfriend because she was a good, loyal girl. However, her parents were not okay with her dating a black man.

This night, I was hanging out with some of my friends who were not a part of the streets. Therefore, I didn't feel the need to have my guns on me this night. We just hung out, drank and smoked some weed. On my way home, I rode past my ex-girlfriend's house and the door was open at 1:30 a.m. I thought it was odd. All the lights were on. I pulled into the driveway and saw a car that was unfamiliar. So, I walked into the house. I made my way slowly through the kitchen and into the living room, without a clue as to what I was about to see.

My heart dropped when I saw my ex sitting on the floor, smoking a joint, with two guys I did not know. It was like a movie scene. All I saw were the heads of two guys turning toward me. She started screaming like in a horror movie. I guess I'd startled them.

I said to myself, *I'd better get out of here quickly.* So, I turned around and walked to my truck as fast as I could;

even stumbling. I didn't know if the guys were cool or if they'd want to start some trouble.

I remember being so mad about leaving my guns at home. All I could think about was killing someone. I was so angry and upset. I kept thinking about having told her not to disrespect me, ever. Now I felt like she had crossed the point of no return. I am so thankful now that I did not have my gun on me that night.

According to research done by the Violence Policy Center in 2013, 94 percent of the women killed by men in their study were murdered by men they knew. Of the victims who knew their offenders, 62 percent were wives or other intimate acquaintances of their killers.

It's important to take notice, what I am talking about right now is real and happens all too frequently in our world today. So there I was — mad because I felt so disrespected, and all I could think about was murder. I have always been a thinker, so I said to myself, *If you are going to kill her, don't stop there. You can do life for one murder.* So, I started thinking of other people that I had forgiven for being disrespectful and launched a plan to kill them as well. If it wasn't for God, I think my life could have played out on an episode of criminal minds. Most of my friends would've told you Bear wasn't like that. However, people never really know what a person is dealing with on the inside. Unless you open up about your feelings, they're in the dark. In the streets, we don't talk about how we feel. Now, after 10 years of being in the streets I realized that I wasn't trying to fit in anymore. I had become a street person and I did not like the direction my life was headed. How many times has someone done something crazy, and when the media interviewed their neighbors they only to hear nothing but good things about the accused. That's exactly what would have been the case for me too; for real.

There I was, angry, bitter, feeling disrespected, and thinking, *Is it okay for me to just start killing people?* In my mind, it was, but I couldn't stop thinking about my parents, especially my mother. My mom and I were really close, and I knew she loved me. She was a cancer survivor, and the last thing I wanted to do was to hurt her.

All I could see in my head was her coming to visit me in prison and saying, "You couldn't do better than this with your life?" For a few days, I replayed that scene several times in my head. I thought about how my parents were God-fearing people and faithful in church. I saw how good their life was compared to mine. My dad was a man. I knew he would be hurt, but he would have done what men do.. He would have adjusted, but not my mom. She would have been devastated. I thank God for the foundation that was laid in my life. If it wasn't for that foundation I would have been in trouble. I would not have known that I can pray to God. I am a living witness that God hears our prayers if we are willing to put in the work.

I believe God gives everyone a chance to change the course of their lives. Most of the time, people are too high, drunk, blind or stubborn to see their chance. Fortunately for me, I was so angry I didn't feel like getting high. I knew that, if I was going to avoid going to prison, this was my only chance.

So, I started praying to see if God was real or not. I didn't know if He could help me. My prayer went like this: "God, if You can hear me. If You are real. I need Your help right now. I am about to do something really stupid and I can't stop myself. It's like it's already done. The handwriting is already on the wall." This was my destiny — to be a killer. It's like I had been living for this moment, and the time had finally come for me to really kill someone. I always thought it would happen and it was just my time. I said, "God, if You can take this anger away from me and there is a possibility for me to do something different, please help me. Because the thoughts I am having right now are insane."

In the greatest book ever written, the author says, "For as he thinketh in his heart, so is he." My thoughts had turned me into a man I did not like. No way did I want to go to prison — for domestic violence or any other crime.

I could be wrong, but I think we were suffering from mental illness because our thoughts were on murder all the time. Somehow, people today think being foolish is cool. People are okay with being known as crazy, wild and irresponsible.

It had become my lifestyle. The only positive thing I was doing with my life was working and paying my bills. Everything I was doing or about to do would have surprised those who loved me. I was consumed with the desire to kill. All they had to do was give me a reason. I was overpowered with anger. At that point, everything I saw and did was affected. Deep down, I really did not want to kill anyone. But because of the lifestyle I chose to live I was consumed with this desire. So, I had no choice but to pray.

We can debate this, but I believe God heard my prayer. To my surprise, a lady who was a friend of my mother's and who knew God came over to our house about four weeks after I prayed that prayer. She gave my mother some preaching cassettes for me to listen to that were on the subject of the spirit of rejection. I laughed, but I listened to the cassettes.And I actually felt better. Then, a pastor from the neighborhood, started coming by my house to invite me to church. I told my mom to tell him I was cool. I wasn't trying to go to church.

One Saturday morning, I went to smoke a joint and to get something to eat. Turning down my street, I saw the preacher on my porch. I was mad because I felt like he was messing up my high. I told him I wasn't interested in coming to church, but he was persistent. So, eventually, I went.

That choice changed my life.

Angelina Jolie said, "Make bold choices, and make bold mistakes." It's all those things that add up to the person you become. I made a bold choice to go to church after all the mistakes I had made in my life. Within a year, I stopped selling drugs, doing drugs, carousing, and cursing. I was cautious of who I spent time with.

Best of all, I stopped thinking about killing people. It was at the church that I learned how to love, forgive, and control my anger. To my surprise, my thoughts started to change. Some might ask, "All of this happened just from reading and hearing the Bible being preached?" It was way more than just reading and listening. What happened in my life was that I started *doing* what I was reading and hearing. More importantly, I believed. What I have learned is that it is impossible to please God without faith. If you desire to see change in your life, you must believe even when you don't understand or agree. When my thoughts changed, guess what? *I* changed.

I don't believe it is a coincidence that I am not locked up or dead. The only reason I shared all these stories with you is so that you can see the type of person that I was and the kinds of people I was hanging around .

It's amazing that I am the man that I am today compared to what I used to do. This wasn't a few incidents or a few bad decisions — this was my lifestyle. I went from trying to fit in to becoming El Oso, Bear, for real. We weren't playing in the streets. People were dying and getting locked up all the time. You could lose your life real quick by putting your hands on somebody like me. Notice I said putting your hands on someone like me. Today, people lose their lives for some foolish reasons. I am glad I was wise enough then and now to know that you don't just kill people for something they say or how they look at you or how you feel. But if my life was in danger or the persons with me, then we would have a problem.

I learned so much from my cousin and my friends. Listening to Tupac everyday, all day, didn't exactly help my thought process. It used to be a few, but now many understand my ambition as a rider. Everybody in the streets or claiming to live that life isn't really true to the streets or the codes. I was really about that life. We tried hard to follow the rules. I hung around some real cats who really did live the street life. To tell you the truth, I still have friends in the streets and I want better for them too. We have too many in the streets who don't understand the game. They don't realize how real it is out there. Many of them, like myself 20 years ago, don't realize the consequences are real and hard to overcome once you cross certain lines.

The street life was the life I desired but that life wasn't taking me where I wanted to be in my life. Today I am no longer living life merely surviving. I have the opportunity now to invest in others.

If I can change, anybody can change. Please don't misunderstand me: What I have been able to accomplish is not easy. It is a challenge to leave the street life. It's not easy to live life sober and deal with people. Many who have tried to get out of the street life have failed.

We have too many good kids, like me, falling victim to these streets. So many are born into this environment and find it hard to escape. Yes, the task is laborious — but it's not impossible.

We have a widespread outbreak of violence that needs to stop. If we want to see a decrease in violence, we must deal with the real problem. The real problem we have today is not guns but people. People do not want to change. I get it, because change is hard.

I had to change my routine and the people I was spending time with. I have been blessed to be able to teach both youth and adults that change is possible, if we believe. I made a choice to change, and the decision was challenging, but now I am grateful for the change.

I have given you only a glimpse of what I've been through that could have changed the course of my life forever. I don't think it's fair for me to live the life that I am living and for the world to be the way it is today. We have too many young people dying in these streets and way too many locked up or headed in that direction.

In Chapter 20, I will share with you part of my routine that changed my life and you can do the same thing to produce a change in your life as well. Whether you are in the streets or not, change is good and my routine can help you.

"One of the greatest decisions a man or a woman can make in their lifetime is to never stop growing as an individual."
— Shawn Moore

20

CHANGE

I am going to use the title of each chapter to sum up my thoughts in this one paragraph about this book. The world we live in today is very *dangerous*, and we are faced with tough decisions daily. Every day, we make *decisions* about when to get up, what to wear, what to eat, where to go, what to do, where to live, and much more. We make decisions that are *dumb, crazy,* or even *illogical*. We take *chances* we should not take. We do things we should not do. Each decision we make comes with *real* consequences. Being on time makes others view you as *reliable*. Wearing a tuxedo to a pool party makes others view you as *ridiculous*. What we hold *close* to our hearts or who we consider as *friends* influences our decisions. The decisions of others affect us, too. The world you live in may leave with you without *hope* because of the *outrageous* things happening around you. You may think no one is *loyal* because you've seen *betrayal* too many times. How can you feel safe and *protected* when your own *family* often lets you down because of *foolish* decisions? It can all drive you *insane*! If that is how you are feeling — lost, desperate, and alone — then it is time for a *change*, regardless of your circumstances and despite what you have done and what you see around you. Change is possible if only you make the decision to believe.

I'm giving you thirteen keys that I learned and that I've lived that have led me to a successful life. Change requires hard work and determination. But if you commit to these keys, I can guarantee that you will not stay the same.

1. *Find a mentor, and trust their advice.* Follow someone who is doing something positive with their life. Even though you may find such a person of integrity, you must realize that your mentor is not perfect. Learn from them anyway — the good and the bad. You cannot be a good leader until you have learned how to follow.

2. *Fight your way through failure because you will mess up sometimes.* Failing is a part of life. Don't quit, and don't give up.

3. *Forget what negative people say to you or about you.* If you can't forget it, use it for motivation to succeed.

4. *Finish what you start.* Don't quit until you accomplish your goal. So many give up way too soon. This quote is hanging up in my office. "OBSTACLES ARE WHAT YOU SEE WHEN YOU TAKE YOUR EYES OFF THE GOAL." — Vince Lombardi

5. ***Stay focused and faithful.*** Consistency and discipline are two keys to success.

6. ***Faith in God must be your foundation for everything you do.*** Without faith, we are in trouble. Put God first, and trust Him. It is better to put your trust in God rather than man.

7. ***Find new friends.*** Don't look down on your old friends, but find new friends.

8. ***Read at least 30 minutes a day.*** I was reading about 4 hours a day in the beginning of my transition. Two hours of that time was reading my Bible.

9. ***Fellowship with like-minded family members.*** Family should be important to you.

10. ***Forgive people.*** Holding on to grudges will only hinder your progress. Let go of the past. Focus on your future, not your past. Develop a strong prayer life. Talk to God about your future. Spend at least 15 minutes a day in prayer preferably more.

11. ***Find a legitimate job, or create one.*** Do whatever it takes to keep it until you find a better one. When you start off, don't worry about the pay. Some money is better than no money.

12.   ***Find a church that is preaching the gospel of Jesus Christ.*** There will be no real change apart from a relationship with God through the person of Jesus Christ. A real man of God will help you in this life and prepare you for the one to come. There is absolutely nothing wrong with being prosperous, but we are not staying here. This is not our home. We need to find a man of God who teaches doctrine and knows the difference between exegesis and eisegesis. Encourage your Pastor to learn the difference. Everyone should keep growing.

13. ***Finally, strive for excellence in everything you do.*** Do your best. Keep your word. Do what you say, meaning don't say and don't do. Your reputation will follow you. Your reputation will open doors for you or close them. Respect the opinion of others, but don't live by them.

I no longer live life controlled by my emotions. My anger issues could have landed me in prison for a long time. Someone has got to teach the next generation about hope, love, and forgiveness. I've learned about these subjects in church. Now that I have 18 years of experience, I am willing to disperse what I have learned. Follow me on Facebook at Shawn Moore Ministries and shawnmooreministries.com

Transformations do happen. I have been transformed for the last 18 years, but the life that I am living today is not just for me. I recently took a class in CPR (cardiopulmonary resuscitation — how to save someone's life). The instructor told us how the American Heart Association made a decision to change how CPR was administered and how that one decision has improved the success rate in saving lives.

Right now everyone is talking about "Stop the Violence," but no one is willing to address the real issue.

I titled this book *El Oso No More* because I truly am a different man today. My friends will tell you I am no longer the "Bear" that they knew. I still have a lot of issues, but nothing like 18 years ago. If we want to see the violence decrease, we must get these kids back in church. We must stop this anti-God movement. We must realize that change is possible only through faith. I put my trust in a God that I could not see, and He changed my life.

I am telling you that someone was deceiving me and trying to destroy my life by constantly trying to get me to kill people. I realize everyone didn't have the opportunity to grow up like I did. Many today have been born into some messed up situations. I am asking you to think on a higher level. There has got to be some evil being behind the scenes pushing people to kill one another. It's evil that makes one unconcerned about being locked up and dying young.

I am challenging you to do what I did in 1998. Weigh your options. Ask yourself where is your life headed and can you do something different?

I am here to tell you like Les Brown says, "It is possible."

One day I was reminiscing and God said to me, "Shawn, the only reason you are where you are today is because of your faith. There is no difference between you and others apart from the fact that you believe. " Faith is powerful. In 1979 a lady came to my house and told me about the gospel of Jesus Christ and I believed and confessed. I didn't understand completely, but I believed.

Look at how my life has turned out compared to so many who refuse to believe and obey God. I don't believe it's a coincidence. I am not saying that if you have faith you can't die young or get locked up. It's just that the odds are against you when you are not making wise decisions. Don't believe this hype that says the Bible is not for the black man. I am a black man whose life has been transformed by the God of the Bible.

The church was a large part of the civil right movement. Don't be surprised if the movement for change comes from the church despite the problems that need to be addressed with the church as well. The church is not perfect, but neither is the world. We haven't left the world, so why try to justify leaving the church?

The majority of our world's problems today like racism, hatred, injustice, murder, rape, lack of respect and love for people, jealousy, envy and a disregard for human life stems from a generation that does not know God. There is no desire to live life by God's standards.

One of the core teachings in the church is love. Right now, the world and the church need to learn a lot more about this single subject.

For those who say, I don't need God and think that it's cool living the street life I offer the following the ancient text says it is appointed unto men once to die, but after this the judgment. How will you be judged? I am praying for you. I hope that you make the right choice to live a life of faith before you take your last breath. A life without God involved can be frustrating, disappointing, empty, idle, pointless, and often times ineffective. I was 28 years old when I decided to change. It's never too late to do something different with your life. Ultimately, the decision is yours but I have to say that my life has been much better with God's involvement. What about your life? The future is bright for the individual who decides it's time to change. –Shawn Moore

REFERENCES

INTRODUCTION

o Rosa Parks quotes, www.bing.com/images, www.quotesgram.com

o Jack Canfield, Chicken Soup for the Soul Publishing, Health Communications, Inc.

o Michael Jordan quote, www.bing.com/images, www.inspirational-picture-quotes.com

o "I can accept failure"

o www.bing.com/images, www.quotesgram.com

o "I've missed more than 9,000 shots."

o Statistic: Feminist Majority Foundation, Feminist.org

CHAPTER 1

o Brian Tracy quote, www.brainyquote.com

o United States Census, www.govtsearches.com/censusbureau

o Les Brown www.Quotefancy

o Looking for love in all the wrong places by Johnnie Lee, www.metrolyrics.com/looking-for-love lyrics-Johnny-lee.html

o www.brainyquotes.com/quotes/robertanthony ID#130323 No Single drop of water thinks

o www.samadhisoft.com/2013/11/23 no-single-rain-drop-think-it-is

- G Batiste https://boardofwisdom.com ID#575769
- www.statisticbrain.com

CHAPTER 2

- www.reference.com/eleanordroose218715-veltquotes

CHAPTER 3

- www.goodread.com/author/quotes/457537.katie_mcgarry

CHAPTER 4

- www.searchquotes.com/quotation/relationships_are_about_trustif
- https://quotes-lover.com/picture-quote/best-friends-are-people-you

CHAPTER 5

- https://www.goodreads.com quotes 218715-make-some-body-happy-today
- www.brainyquote.com/quotes/bruce.lee ID#383809
- www.lovetravelquotes.com/itsimpossible-saidpride-its-risky

CHAPTER 6

- www.azquotes.com Author Z Z Zigziglar/
- Report by Urban Institute
- www.brainyquote.com/quotes/vladimir_lenin/136307
- www.brainyquotes.com/quotes/quotesgailsheeny ID#158938

o www.brainyquote.com/quotes/mary_tyler_moore ID#130341

o www.goodreads.com/author/quotes/ Naaem_Callaway

CHAPTER 7

o https://quotefance.com/quote/1234074/Herman-Kahn_failures-of

CHAPTER 8

o www.brainyquote.com/quotes/J_donald_walters ID#183437

CHAPTER 9

o www.picturequotes.com/one-stupid-mistake-can-change-everything

o www.brainyquote.com/quotes/toney_robbins ID#147787

o Quotefancy.com/quote/771229/Barack-Obama-Learning-to-stand

CHAPTER 11

o www.decison-points.net

o www.quoteswave.com/picture-quotes/82836

CHAPTER 12

o Simplereminders.com/quotes/good-those-who-those-who-believe

o www.lifehack.org/articles/productivity/difficult-roads-often-lead

o www.searchquotes.com/search/there_no_way_I_was_born_to_just_pay

- www.searchquotes.com/quotation/success_is_99%_attitudeand1
- www.quotationspage.com/quote/38644html(page 96) 2nd paragraph
- www.goodreads.comquotes/69426/change-is-hard-because

CHAPTER 13

- www.picturequotes.com/your-real-friends-will-always-have-your-back

CHAPTER 14

- www.quote.snydle.com

CHAPTER 15

- www.goodreads.com/quotes/375040-everyone-suffers-at-least
- www.quotationspage.com/quote/21097.html
- Martin Luther, www.lovequotes.symphonyoflove.net/martin-luther-king-jr-dr-love-quotes
- Tupac, www.goodreads.com/quotes/52533
- Nelson Mandela, www.goodreads.com/quotes/111810/no-one-is-born-hating
- www.quotegee.com/quotes-from-movies/scarface ID#17871

CHAPTER 16

- www.brainyquote.com/quotes/jonathan_swift_384840117

CHAPTER 17

- www.brainyquote.com/quotes/john_wooden_447007

CHAPTER 18

- https://www.brainyquote.com/authors/seth_macfarlane

CHAPTER 19

- www.brainyquote.com/quotes/tony_robbins ID#147787
- Stats Violence Policy www.vpc.org
- Angelina Jolie, www.brainyquote.com/quotes/angelina_jolie_644376

CHAPTER 20

- Les Brown, www.fearlessmotivation.com